WATTS
COOKING

DELICIOUSLY SIMPLE RECIPES
TO INSPIRE HOME COOKS

This book is dedicated to the memory
of my nephew Albie who was taken
from us far too soon.

I'm sure he'd have been just as big
of a foodie as I am.

CONTENTS

MY JOURNEY, IN MY OWN WORDS

I left school at 16 with no idea of what I wanted to do with my life. I felt lost, frustrated, and seeking a sense of purpose. Unfortunately, I found a false sense of purpose in the wrong place and, to cut a long story short, I ended up in prison at the tender age of 18. I was sentenced to six and a half years for grievous bodily harm.

As the heavy steel door slammed behind me, I realised I had to make serious changes if I wanted to have any chance of success in my life. The most likely scenario that faced me was a vicious cycle of reoffending, but from day one I was determined not to be part of those shocking statistics.

I started by changing my attitude as well as my outlook on life. I stopped seeing myself as a victim of the system and took full responsibility for how and why I was in that position.

I took every opportunity that could possibly benefit me, even though my release date felt like it was never going to come. I took part in educational courses in all kinds of subjects, from maths to business studies and even a fitness course.

The thing that ended up having the most profound effect on me was when I started working towards the Duke of Edinburgh's Award. During my time in prison, I became the first person in custody to complete the bronze, silver, and gold awards. The different sections of the award helped to mould my character and saw me grow from a lost young boy to a man with dreams and aspirations. It taught me to be resilient, and it boosted my self-esteem, confidence, and interpersonal skills.

The section of the award that had the biggest impact on me was the Skills section. At the time of choosing my skill, I happened to have a job in the prison kitchen, so the question of which to pick was a no-brainer. As you can imagine, a prison kitchen is not the best environment to learn how to cook. The budget is very low, and I was never sure if the meat was even real! Luckily, I was fortunate enough to get a job in the officer's mess, which was basically the canteen for the prison's staff. Only two inmates worked there at any one time, and they would always be working towards their NVQ qualification. This meant that they would be there for at least a year, so the job didn't come up very often. I quickly realised that this was a fantastic and rare opportunity, so as soon as it became available, I grabbed it with both hands.

I had a natural talent for cooking, but I never thought it would become my career, let alone something I would fall madly in love with. In that little kitchen, I started with the basics, learning everything from knife skills to food health, hygiene, and safety. As far as food goes, it involved making a lot of classic dishes. Things like shepherd's pie, lasagne, toad in the hole, apple crumble, and lemon tarts to name just a few. Although it was nothing like the main prison kitchen, the budget was still tight. Every so often, however, something exciting would appear, and we would have the opportunity to learn a new skill. I remember a whole salmon turning up one day which needed preparing – everything from descaling to filleting it.

Towards the latter stages of my sentence, and once I had finished the cookery qualification, I was able to move to a resettlement unit. From this unit, I could be temporarily released for work. All my hard work and dedication so far had paid off, and I was delighted when head chef Ian Nagelson offered me the opportunity to work in one of Jamie Oliver's restaurants.

It was here that a fire was lit inside of me, one that is still raging today. The adrenaline rush of being in a busy kitchen environment is one that is not easily matched. I was in awe as I watched the experienced chefs at work. They were all bursting with passion for what they were doing, and it rubbed off on me.

We mostly used dried herbs in the prison, and to this day I vividly remember the smell of the fresh herbs hitting me on my first day at the restaurant. My eyes lit up as I entered the fridge and saw and smelt almost every herb you could imagine. The vegetables, too, were amazing. I had grown up hating beetroot as I was used to the pickled stuff that my nan always put on the table, but here I was looking at golden beets with their deep yellow colour and candied beets with their bold white and pink rings. They were so beautiful. I also saw a celeriac for the very first time, and I couldn't help but think it looked like a little brain. Even the tomatoes amazed me. At that point in my life, I had only known tomatoes to be red, yet here I was preparing heritage tomatoes of all different shapes, colours and sizes. I quickly discovered the impact the quality of the produce has on the taste. It was love at first sight.

I spent the next ten months learning everything I could about being a professional chef. I was so lucky to have some incredibly supportive mentors around me that took me under their wings. Without them, I would have undoubtedly failed. They taught me a good work ethic, and I was always the first to arrive at the kitchen in my freshly ironed chef whites, ready for the day ahead. Every single day was just as exciting as the last.

In April 2011, two weeks before my release from prison, I was awarded the Duke of Edinburgh's Gold Award at St James's Palace in London. It was the proudest moment of my life, and I felt like I had proven my worth not only to myself but to everybody that I'd let down only a few years before. I had the honour of meeting HRH Prince Philip and talking to him about my experience of working towards achieving the award. As it turned out, I had also proven my worth in the restaurant as I was offered a full-time job upon my release. You can only imagine my pride as I started work as a free man just two days after walking out of the prison gates.

I went on to work for Jamie's restaurants for five more years. During this time, my hunger for learning was so great that on my days off I would work for free in some of the country's best restaurants, just to learn what I could.

In 2016, I ventured out on my own. I started by buying a food truck and serving healthy lunch options on St Albans high street. I also catered for private events, from small dinner parties to weddings and everything in between. I quickly gained a reputation that saw me accepting some incredible opportunities. At the end of 2016, I was the chef in the X Factor house, and in that same year, I had my first taste of cooking on screen when I featured in two advertising campaigns for Quorn. As well as these experiences, I've cooked in some amazing places, including Windsor Castle. I have held corporate contracts and events contracts – all of which have given me the freedom to be creative – and many of my clients have been well-known celebrities and even royalty.

In 2020, with the coronavirus pandemic disrupting business, I took to social media to share my passion. I was blown away by how well my recipes were received and how popular they were becoming. I was able to grow a loyal foodie following just by sharing my passion for food and life. Then, in April 2021, ten years to the day after being released from prison, my newfound exposure led to me achieving one of my dreams: I cooked live on ITV's This Morning in front of over one million viewers.

I could very easily hide away from my past, but it's an important part of why I am who I am today. Over the last few years, I've spent time mentoring young people as well as talking and teaching in prisons and schools. I've seen how much telling my story can motivate and inspire – not just young people, but people from all walks of life.

I hope this helps you understand my burning desire to share some of the amazing recipes that my journey has inspired. I've been overwhelmed by how many people have been making my recipes since I started creating them – a lot of whom had never tried baking or cooking before.

Inspiring people to cook gives me a powerful sense of fulfillment. Since I first started sharing recipes on social media, I've been moved by how many messages I've received from people saying how recreating my recipes has changed their lives. When creating a recipe, I am always thinking about how I can make them easy and accessible for the everyday cook. I really enjoy taking classic, notoriously difficult recipes and making them simple – even for a beginner.

In this book, you'll find some of the recipes that have helped me to establish myself as one of the most influential social media chefs. You'll also find lots of brand new and exclusive recipes, including some that I've been saving especially for this book. Enjoy, and don't forget to let me know how you get on!

STORE CUPBOARD ESSENTIALS

If you cook often, you're sure to find yourself using the same cupboard ingredients over and over again. Stocking up on the essentials means you'll always have access to key ingredients, saving on endless trips to the shops.

There are loads of benefits to having a well-stocked kitchen. Most importantly, making dishes that use these ingredients can help prevent food waste as well as save you time and money. So, here's my list of the most essential store cupboard items.

TINS

CHOPPED TOMATOES
The foundation for so many sauces, soups, stews, and casseroles – the truest essential.

BEANS AND PULSES
Chickpeas, cannellini beans, kidney beans, butter beans, and lentils are all great fillers and bulkers, as well as excellent sources of protein and fibre.

COCONUT MILK
Add it to soups and curries for a mellow, creamy flavour.

STARCHY FOODS

POTATOES
Maris Piper or King Edward potatoes are great all-rounders. Potatoes are super versatile and can be made into all kinds of wonderful side dishes.

RICE (BASMATI OR LONG GRAIN)
A top pairing for spicy sauces and curries. You can find tips on how to make perfectly fluffy rice in my tips and advice section (see page 18).

DRIED PASTA
Ideal for pasta bakes, stovetop wonders, and even soups and salads. Stock a few different pasta shapes, from spaghetti to fusilli, to mix up your midweek meals.

DRIED NOODLES (EGG OR RICE)
Great for stir fries, soups, and curries.

JARS AND BOTTLES

VEGETABLE OIL AND SUNFLOWER OIL
A classic neutral oil that's perfect for everyday cooking.

EXTRA VIRGIN OLIVE OIL
For dressing salads and drizzling over finished dishes – never cooking.

TOASTED SESAME OIL
A deliciously nutty oil that's often used in Southeast Asian cuisine. Use for flavouring, not for frying.

HONEY
Adds a touch of sweetness to sauces and marinades.

MUSTARD (WHOLEGRAIN AND DIJON)
Adds a bit of a kick to stews, sauces and marinades, but can also be used as a condiment.

SOY SAUCE (LIGHT OR DARK)

Adds a richness and saltiness to many marinades and sauces. Use the lower salt varieties whenever possible.

VINEGARS (RED WINE, CIDER AND BALSAMIC)

Lots of dishes benefit from the acidity of vinegar – think dressings, marinades, sauces and stews.

WORCESTERSHIRE SAUCE

Great for adding depth and an umami flavour to stews and casseroles.

HERBS AND SPICES

SALT AND BLACK PEPPER

Used in almost every meal; an absolute essential when it comes to seasoning to taste.

SMOKED PAPRIKA

Punchy, smoky goodness made from dried red peppers.

GROUND CUMIN

Robust and earthy in flavour, this spice is an integral part of traditional Indian cooking.

DRIED OREGANO

Think Mediterranean vibes - fresh and fragrant. This herb is also an essential flavour in Italian American cuisine.

CHILLI

Whether flakes, powder, mild or hot… we all need a bit of spice in our lives!

GROUND CINNAMON

A warming and comforting flavour. Great for both sweet and savoury bakes and sauces.

GROUND CORIANDER

Lemony and fragrant. Another classic in Indian cuisine.

CURRY POWDER

A warming blend of spices used for basic sauces and curries.

CHINESE FIVE SPICE

A fabulous mixture of star anise, cloves, cinnamon, Szechuan peppercorns and fennel seeds. This is a fantastic addition to marinades, rubs and Asian dishes.

MISCELLANEOUS

GOOD-QUALITY STOCK CUBES OR POTS

A wonderful way to add depth of flavour and seasoning to loads of different dishes.

FLOUR (PLAIN FLOUR, SELF-RAISING FLOUR AND CORNFLOUR)

For thickening sauces, baking, and making fried meat, fish and veggies extra crispy.

TOMATO PASTE

Adds a concentrated, intense tomato flavour as well as helping to thicken sauces.

SUGAR (GOLDEN AND WHITE CASTER SUGAR, GRANULATED SUGAR, AND SOFT BROWN SUGAR)

Used for baking but can also add a balance of sweetness to some savoury dishes.

TIPS & ADVICE

OILS

WHY DO GOOD COOKING OILS MATTER?

When cooking oils are heated, particularly at high temperatures, they eventually reach their smoke point. The smoke point is the temperature at which the oil is no longer stable and begins to break down. When oils break down, they can create an unpleasant burnt taste, as well as pose a risk to your health.

HERE'S A LIST OF POPULAR OILS AND WHAT THEY'RE GOOD FOR:

EXTRA VIRGIN OLIVE OIL

Quite possibly the most well-known and frequently used oil, extra virgin olive oil has earned its reputation as a healthy, versatile oil. Its low smoke point, however, means it's not the best oil to use for cooking. For this reason, extra virgin olive oil is recommended for dips and dressing, or for adding a finishing touch to pastas and other dishes.

LIGHT OLIVE OIL

Extra virgin may get the most attention in the world of olive oils, but its lighter cousin contains many of the same health-boosting properties. Light olive oil has a far higher smoke point of about 240°c, therefore it's ideal for high-temperature cooking, like sautéing, roasting, and grilling.

Light olive oil can also be used in baking but beware as its flavour may be overpowering. Don't be fooled by its name, either! This olive oil doesn't contain fewer calories than other varieties – 'light' simply refers to its colour and more neutral taste.

SUNFLOWER AND OTHER VEGETABLE OIL

The refining process of both sunflower and vegetable oil leaves them with a neutral taste and medium-high smoke point of 205°c. This makes them useful for stir frying, sautéing, grilling, frying, and baking. These are the two oils that I most commonly cook with.

AVOCADO OIL

If you know that avocados are chock-full of healthy fats, you won't be surprised to learn that their oil is too. Not only this, but avocado oil also boasts the highest known smoke point of any plant oil: 270°c for refined and up to 250°c for unrefined (also known as virgin). It's perfect for frying, searing, roasting, and grilling.

COCONUT OIL

Like most other oils, coconut comes in two varieties: refined and unrefined. Refined coconut oil has a smoke point of 230°c and works well for sautéing or roasting. It has a light coconut taste and is the more neutral of the two varieties. Unrefined coconut oil, on the other hand, offers a more signature coconut flavour, and is best used for colder dishes in the same way as extra virgin olive oil.

SESAME OIL (NOT TO BE CONFUSED WITH TOASTED SESAME OIL)

Sesame oil may just be the unsung hero our cooking needs (and it might even rival olive oil as a healthy cooking option.) A mid-range smoke point of anywhere from 175°c to 205°c means it can be used in stir frying and sautéing, and its slight nutty flavour makes it perfect for drizzling, too.

Toasted sesame oil is almost an entirely different ingredient; it has a strong flavour and works well as a flavour enhancer in some Asian-style dishes.

POTATOES

Have you ever stood in the supermarket and wondered which potatoes to choose? With so many varieties available, it's hard to know which one will work best for your dish, so here's a guide to the different types of potatoes and what they're best suited to. You'll never be stuck again!

POTATOES ARE CATEGORISED INTO THREE BASIC TYPES: FLOURY (STARCHY), WAXY, AND ALL-ROUNDERS.

FLOURY

Floury potatoes are high in starch, low in moisture, and have a floury texture with a creamy white flesh. Starchy potatoes release a milky, starchy liquid if pricked or cut.

VARIETIES OF FLOURY POTATOES:

Maris Piper

King Edward

Russets

Sweet potatoes

WHEN TO USE:

Floury potatoes are fluffy and absorbent which makes them great for baking and frying. Try using them to make crispy potatoes, chips, wedges, or hash browns. They can also be mashed, but they'll become stodgy if overworked.

WHEN TO AVOID:

Due to their high starch content, floury potatoes don't hold together well when cooked, so avoid using them in dishes that require boiling, roasting or slicing, like casseroles, potato gratins or potato salads.

WAXY

Waxy potatoes have less starch than floury potatoes and contain more moisture and sugar. They are often smaller with a waxy outer skin and a creamy, firm, and moist flesh.

VARIETIES OF WAXY POTATOES INCLUDE:

Charlotte

Jersey Royals

New potatoes

Baby potatoes

Vivaldi

La Ratte

Cornish Kings

WHEN TO USE:

Waxy potatoes hold their shape well after cooking, so are great for boiling, roasting or slicing. Use them for potato salads, or add them to stews, casseroles, and soups.

WHEN TO AVOID:

Waxy potatoes are not good for mashing because they hold their shape and produce a chunky mash. Also avoid them when baking or deep frying.

ALL-ROUNDERS

All-rounder potatoes have a medium starch content that falls somewhere in between floury and waxy potatoes. They have more moisture than floury potatoes and hold their shape in boiling water.

VARIETIES:

Red potatoes

Osprey

Desiree

British white potatoes

Yukon Gold

WHEN TO USE:

All-rounder potatoes are particularly useful for roasting, pan frying, and stewing and make good gratins such as potato dauphinoise.

WHEN TO AVOID:

They can be baked, mashed, or deep fried like a floury potato, but will not produce the same fluffy texture. You can use all-rounder potatoes for just about anything, but if you have a specific dish in mind that lends itself to a floury or waxy potato, then go for those types instead.

RICE

Rice is one of the most consumed foods in the world and for good reason. It's versatile, substantial, easy to prepare, and delicious, making it a perfect staple in every kitchen. Whether it's incorporated into a main dish or served as a side, rice can do it all while providing comfort and fullness.

SHORT, MEDIUM, AND LONG GRAIN: WHAT'S THE DIFFERENCE?

Rice grains come in three sizes: short, medium, and long grain. Short grain rice, like risotto's arborio rice, or paella's bomba rice, are similar in length and width and take on a sticky texture when cooked. Medium grain rice is about twice as long as it is wide and becomes moist and tender when cooked. Long grain rice, like jasmine rice and basmati rice, is anywhere from three to four times as long as it is wide and takes on a drier, fluffy texture when cooked.

HERE ARE SIX COMMON KINDS OF RICE, THEIR DISTINCTIONS, AND THE BEST WAYS TO ENJOY THEM.

BASMATI RICE

Basmati rice is native to India, where more than 70% of the world's basmati is produced. Basmati rice works best in dishes like pilaf or biryani or as a side to curries and stews.

WHOLEGRAIN RICE

Also known as brown rice, wholegrain rice is a lot like white rice, but hasn't had as much of the grain removed. The only part that's removed from brown rice is the outer hull, which is inedible. White rice, on the other hand, has the outer hull, germ, and bran removed, and is polished once the milling process is complete. Therefore, brown rice has a denser texture, nuttier flavour, and higher nutritional value, including much more fibre and iron. It's super versatile and makes a healthier substitute wherever white rice is used.

ARBORIO RICE

Arborio rice is a short grain Italian white rice. It's best known for being risotto's go-to grain. It's rich in amylopectin starch, so when it's cooked, arborio rice becomes chewy, firm, and creamy all at once, making it the perfect vehicle for other rich dishes, like rice pudding.

JASMINE RICE

Jasmine rice is a long grain rice that's known for its mild, sweet flavour. Primarily grown in Southeast Asia, jasmine rice is a staple in Thai and Cambodian cuisine. Jasmine rice, especially white jasmine rice, takes on a slightly sticky texture when cooked and is usually served steamed.

BOMBA RICE

This nearly spherical short grain rice, also known as Valencia rice, is cultivated in Spain and is the preferred variety for paella. Bomba rice is highly absorbent and requires more water to cook. It also has a high starch content, meaning it tends not to stick to the pan during cooking.

WILD RICE

Wild rice isn't exactly rice, but it's the term used for the grain that's produced by a certain type of grass native to North America and China. Wild rice is more difficult to cultivate and harvest than true rice. It has a tougher texture, but it's a good source of protein, B vitamins, and lysine, an amino acid used in the biosynthesis of proteins. Wild rice is commonly used in salads.

HERE ARE EIGHT TIPS TO HELP YOU COOK THE PERFECT POT OF RICE EVERY TIME.

Get to know your rice varieties: some are fluffy, some are sticky, and they can't really be substituted for one another.

The most common cooking ratio for rice is two parts water to one part rice. This doesn't work perfectly for every single variety of rice though.

Some rice varieties require rinsing before you cook them. Basmati rice, for example, needs rinsing to prevent it from becoming sticky and clumping together.

It's fine to stir the rice when you first add it to the water, but then you need to leave it alone. Unless, of course, it's risotto rice and you want to help release all its creamy, starchy goodness.

If you're cooking on the stove, use a heavy-bottomed pot to prevent the rice from burning.

Make sure you season it with salt.

During the final stages of cooking, place a kitchen towel underneath the lid to absorb any condensation and prevent the rice from getting mushy.

Once your rice is cooked, let it rest for about 15 minutes before eating it. Just fluff it up with a fork before serving.

PASTA

How many types of pasta can you name? Spaghetti, lasagne, penne, fusilli…. they're some of the easy ones. It'd be a bit tricky to name all of them when there are over 300 varieties though!

So how are there so many, and what's the difference? Firstly, there's the shape: everything from long and thin to short and fat, ribbons, bows, tubes, sheets, shells, and more. Then there's the ingredients: whole wheat, buckwheat, durum wheat, semolina, rice, eggs – there are plenty of variations. There's also colour and texture, but perhaps the most influential factor when it comes to identifying pasta is where it comes from.

Pasta has been a staple part of the Italian diet for centuries, and as the nation has evolved, so have the recipes, with many regions having their own unique take on pasta. The specialty in Piemonte, for example, is agnolotti, which are squares of pasta with a meat or vegetable filling. Southern Sardinia, on the other hand, has culurgioni, which is traditionally filled with ricotta cheese, egg and saffron, and shaped like a wheat tip. Meanwhile, in parts of northern Italy, they tuck into strozzapreti which, if translated literally, means "strangled priests". Rumour has it the priests would gobble these up so enthusiastically they'd choke, hence the name.

However many types of pasta you know, the chances are you've got your own special way of serving it and making it your own. If you do, then congratulations – nothing could be more Italian than doing it your own way!

HERE ARE SOME POPULAR SHAPES OF PASTA AND WHAT THEY'RE BEST USED FOR.

SPAGHETTI

Who doesn't love spaghetti? It's probably the most-cooked pasta in the UK. Though spaghetti and meatballs is one of the most classic combinations, this pasta works best with light seafood sauces and cream or oil-based sauces. Spaghetti is perhaps best known for being paired with a bolognese sauce, but it's entirely inauthentic and sure to anger a few Italians!

PENNE

Penne is likely a family favourite in your kitchen. It's a hollow cylindrical pasta with slanted edges. Its distinct ridges make it perfect for catching sauce, and it's a versatile pasta shape that's an absolutely essential store cupboard ingredient.

TAGLIATELLE

It's easy to get tagliatelle and fettuccine mixed up. In fact, in some parts of Italy, cooks refer to tagliatelle as fettucine. Both types of pasta look like flattened spaghetti and are a similar width, but tagliatelle provides a slightly thicker bite. It handles thick meat sauces well, but it'll do a cream or tomato sauce justice, too.

RIGATONI

Rigatoni looks like penne's big brother. It's also cylindrical with slight ridges, but it's slightly stumpier, wider, and it doesn't have slanted edges. Like penne, the ridges and hollow centre are amazing at trapping sauce.

BUCATINI

This is my personal favourite pasta shape. It looks a lot like traditional spaghetti, but it's rounder with a hollow centre, making it a little thicker than spaghetti. When cooked in soups, pasta dishes, or casseroles, it hoards extra sauce in its centre. That's the superpower of bucatini.

CAVATAPPI

This hollow, spiral-shaped pasta is also referred to as double elbow pasta. The multiple twists and turns increase its surface area, making it another great sauce trap. It's a firm favourite when making macaroni cheese.

LINGUINE

Linguine resembles fettuccine, but it's not as wide. It's commonly paired with seafood dishes, marrying perfectly with clams and mussels. In fact, when it comes to linguine, any cream-based or white wine sauce is a match made in heaven.

FUSILLI

This spiral-shaped noodle has a lot of grooves and crevices to catch extra sauce and dressings. It's sturdy enough to toss with a thicker sauce like marinara or a meat sauce, but it's also perfect for on-the-go pasta salads.

PAPPARDELLE

Pappardelle pasta is like a wider version of tagliatelle, so it's even better with rich, meat-based sauces. It's big, bad, and sturdy, so you can throw any hearty sauce its way. Most commonly, you'll see it paired with a ragù or bolognese sauce.

FARFALLE

It sounds exotic, but farfalle is simply everyone's favourite bow tie pasta. You'll find it in all types of creamy sauces as well as pasta salads. There's not a lot you can't do with this type of pasta.

SPEEDY WEEKNIGHT DINNERS

These are the meals that I'm known for: delicious dishes which use easily accessible ingredients and take less than 30 minutes to make. A lot of these recipes contain ingredients that most of us already have in our kitchen cupboards, so you won't have to spend a lot of money chasing down various ingredients.

This chapter is full of perfect, flavourful midweek dinners that will help you fall in love with cooking.

CHICKEN STROGANOFF

PREP TIME: 5 MINUTES | COOKING TIME: 10 MINUTES | SERVES: 2

This chicken version of the classic beef stroganoff is sure to be a crowd pleaser. Although using chicken saves money, it sure doesn't skimp on flavour. Super quick and simple to make, this is the perfect recipe to kick off my Speedy Weeknight Dinners.

INGREDIENTS

2 chicken breasts

1 tbsp plain flour

20g butter

1 onion, sliced

250g chestnut mushrooms, quartered

4 cloves of garlic, chopped

200ml chicken stock

180ml crème fraiche

1 tbsp Dijon mustard

15g parsley, chopped

METHOD

1. Cut the chicken into strips and pop them into a bowl. Add the plain flour and season with salt and pepper. Stir well to coat the chicken.

2. Heat a little oil in a large frying pan over a medium to high heat. Add the butter and leave to melt.

3. Once the butter has melted, add the chicken and cook until it's golden-brown all over. Remove from the pan and set aside.

4. Add the onion to the same pan and cook for 4 to 5 minutes until softened.

5. Add the mushrooms and cook for a few more minutes, stirring occasionally.

6. Add the garlic and cook for 1 minute before adding the chicken stock, crème fraiche and Dijon mustard. Stir well.

7. Pop the chicken back into the pan and bring to the boil. Cook until the chicken is cooked through and the sauce has thickened.

8. Season to taste and add the chopped parsley. Serve with rice, mashed potatoes, or pasta.

BACON-WRAPPED PORK TENDERLOIN

PREP TIME: 5 MINUTES | COOKING TIME: 20 MINUTES | SERVES: 2

This is one of those miracle recipes that just happens to only require three ingredients: pork, bacon, and honey. Just sear the pork, roll it up in the bacon, drizzle with honey, and bake. Easy.

INGREDIENTS

8 rashers of streaky bacon

500g pork tenderloin

2 tbsp honey

METHOD

1. Preheat the oven to 200°c.

2. Lay the bacon vertically on a board, with each rasher overlapping slightly. There should be enough bacon that, when rolled up, it will wrap around the length of the pork.

3. Season the pork with salt and pepper, then tuck the thin end of the fillet under so the pork is roughly the same thickness from end to end.

4. Heat some oil in a large pan over a high heat. Sear the pork on all sides until nicely browned. Don't worry about cooking it through as it's going to go into the oven.

5. Remove the seared pork from the pan and leave to cool slightly so you can handle it. Then, place the pork onto the bacon and roll it up to encase the whole tenderloin.

6. Transfer the pork onto a baking tray, drizzle over the honey, and use a brush or your fingers to help coat the pork.

7. Bake for 15 minutes, then take it out of the oven and baste it with the pan juices. Return to the oven and cook for a further 5 minutes.

8. Once cooked, leave to rest for 5 minutes before carving.

9. Serve with some of the juices from the pan and a healthy scoop of Champ Mash (see page 206).

SWEET CHILLI CHICKEN

PREP TIME: 5 MINUTES | COOKING TIME: 10 MINUTES | SERVES: 2

This Sweet Chilli Chicken recipe is super simple and tastes absolutely incredible. I guarantee you're going to have this one on repeat.

INGREDIENTS

2 chicken breasts

2 eggs, lightly beaten

60g plain flour

I tsp garlic paste

I tsp ginger paste

I tbsp soy sauce

I tbsp tomato ketchup

4 tbsp sweet chilli sauce

TO GARNISH (OPTIONAL)

I tsp sesame seeds

2 spring onions, sliced

METHOD

1. Cut the chicken breasts into bite-size chunks, then dip each piece into the beaten eggs, followed by the plain flour. Once each piece is coated, pop them onto a plate and set aside.

2. Heat some oil in a large frying pan and cook the chicken over a medium to high heat until it's golden, crispy, and cooked through. It should take about 5 minutes.

3. Turn the heat down to medium, add the garlic and ginger, and cook for a further minute.

4. Pour in the soy sauce, ketchup, and sweet chilli sauce. Cook until it thickens and starts to turn sticky. If it gets too thick, just add a splash of water.

5. Serve with rice and finish with a sprinkle of sesame seeds and spring onions.

BEEF CHOW MEIN

PREP TIME: 10 MINUTES | COOKING TIME: 10 MINUTES | SERVES: 4

This delicious Beef Chow Mein is perfect when you want something special on a busy weeknight. Ready in under 20 minutes, plus it's tastier and healthier than a takeaway!

INGREDIENTS

FOR THE SAUCE

100ml chicken stock

6 tbsp oyster sauce

3 tbsp soy sauce

3 tbsp sesame oil

1 tbsp cornflour

1 tbsp soft brown sugar

FOR THE CHOW MEIN

150g fine egg noodles

300g sirloin steak, thinly sliced

1 onion, sliced

2 cloves of garlic, chopped

1 carrot, cut into matchsticks

1 pepper, sliced

¼ savoy cabbage, thinly sliced

100g beansprouts

100g spring onions, sliced

Sesame seeds, for garnish

METHOD

1. Cook the noodles as per the packet instructions, then drain and run under cold water to stop them sticking together. Set aside for the moment.

2. Meanwhile, make the chow mein sauce by adding all the sauce ingredients to a bowl and mixing until smooth.

3. Heat a little cooking oil in a large frying pan or a wok over a high heat. Fry the steak strips for 2-3 minutes, turning once or twice, until the steak is just cooked. Remove the steak from the pan and set aside.

4. Add a little more oil to the same pan, then stir fry the onion, garlic and carrot for 2 minutes.

5. Chuck in the pepper, cabbage, beansprouts, and most of the spring onion to stir fry for 2 more minutes.

6. Now put the steak back into the pan along with the noodles. Pour in the chow mein sauce and then stir fry for 2-3 minutes until the noodles are hot.

7. Serve your chow mein topped with the remaining spring onion and sesame seeds.

CHICKEN & PROSCIUTTO MILANESE

PREP TIME: 15 MINUTES | COOKING TIME: 10 MINUTES | SERVES: 2

Exactly ten years after being released from prison, I was invited to cook on ITV's This Morning. It was the very first time I'd done a live cooking demo, and it was on national television for over one million viewers! I still pinch myself when I think back to that surreal moment. When I got the call from Natalie, the food editor, I already knew what I wanted to cook. I had been planning this moment for years; I knew it was coming. I explained to her that I had a vision board full of my goals and ambitions, and that I'd photoshopped myself over a picture of Gino D'Acampo cooking on the set of This Morning. This only made the experience more magical. The dish I made was inspired by the Italian Milanese. Thin, tender chicken breast smothered with garlic butter, topped with gouda cheese, prosciutto and coated in crispy breadcrumbs. Here it is. I'd love you to try it.

INGREDIENTS

3 cloves of garlic, crushed

50g butter, softened

5g parsley, chopped

2 chicken breasts

4 slices of gouda

4 slices of prosciutto

100g plain flour

2 eggs, lightly beaten

200g breadcrumbs

TO SERVE

2 eggs

40g parmesan, grated

A handful of rocket

10ml extra virgin olive oil

1 lemon, juiced

METHOD

1. Mix the garlic, softened butter and chopped parsley together in a small bowl.

2. Fold cling film over itself to create multiple layers. Place one chicken breast onto baking paper, place the cling film on top, then bash with a rolling pin or a meat tenderiser until it has flattened into a thin escalope, about 0.5cm thick.

3. Spread the garlic butter over one side of the chicken, then lay two slices of gouda on top, followed by two slices of prosciutto.

4. Cover with the cling film and bash again to pound the meat and cheese into the chicken breast. Set aside, then repeat with the other piece of chicken.

5. Place the flour into one tray, the beaten eggs into another, and the breadcrumbs into a third.

6. Coat each escalope in the flour, then the egg, and finally in the breadcrumbs.

7. Heat a good amount of oil in a large frying pan over a medium to high heat. Shallow fry the chicken for about 3 to 4 minutes on each side, or until cooked through and golden-brown. Place onto kitchen paper once done to soak up any excess oil.

8. Fry the eggs and serve them on top of each escalope, then finish with a generous grating of parmesan.

9. Dress the rocket leaves with the olive oil and lemon juice and serve on the side.

COCONUT FISH CURRY

PREP TIME: 5 MINUTES | COOKING TIME: 15 MINUTES | SERVES: 2

This colourful one-pot fish curry is inspired by Thai and Indian flavours and makes a wonderfully quick, healthy and fragrant midweek meal.

INGREDIENTS

FOR THE SPICE PASTE

2 tsp turmeric

2 tsp cumin

1 tsp garam masala

½ onion

1 red chilli

2 cloves of garlic

1 tsp ginger paste

1 lime, zested

1 bunch of coriander, stalks and leaves separated

FOR THE CURRY

1 tsp mustard seeds

20g butter

1 x 400ml tin of full-fat coconut milk

1 tbsp soft brown sugar

4 fillets of white fish, such as pollock or cod

1 tsp fish sauce

1-2 limes

METHOD

1. Add the spice paste ingredients, except the coriander leaves, along with one tablespoon of water to a blender and blend until smooth. (The leaves will be used for garnish later.)

2. In a large saucepan, gently toast the mustard seeds until they start to pop, then add the butter and spice paste.

3. Turn up the heat and fry for about a minute, stirring continuously.

4. Pour in the coconut milk, add the soft brown sugar, then simmer for a further 5 minutes.

5. Season the fish with a little salt and pepper. Add it to the sauce, pop on a lid, and gently poach for about 3 to 4 minutes until cooked through.

6. Turn off the heat, then add the fish sauce and squeeze over lots of lime juice.

7. Season to taste and top with the remaining coriander leaves. Serve with rice and broccoli or sautéed pak choi.

CRISPY CHILLI BEEF

PREP TIME: 5 MINUTES | COOKING TIME: 15 MINUTES | SERVES: 2

Fakeaways are becoming increasingly popular, and lots of us are having a go at recreating our favourite takeaway meals at home (and often finding we can do a better job!). This quick Crispy Chilli Beef recipe uses supermarket ingredients to recreate a delicious Chinese takeaway classic.

INGREDIENTS

300g thin cut sirloin

2 tbsp cornflour

1 tbsp Chinese five spice

1 large red pepper, sliced

1 red chilli, sliced

1 bunch of spring onions, sliced

1 handful of beansprouts

2 tsp ginger paste

2 tsp garlic paste

FOR THE SAUCE

3 tbsp rice wine vinegar

2 tbsp soy sauce

2 tbsp tomato ketchup

2 tbsp sweet chilli sauce

METHOD

1. Cut the sirloin into thin strips and place in a bowl with the cornflour and Chinese five spice. Mix well to completely coat the beef.

2. Heat a good amount of oil in a frying pan or a wok, then add the beef and fry over a high heat until it's really crispy.

3. Remove the beef from the pan and place onto kitchen paper to soak up any excess oil.

4. In a clean pan, stir fry the red pepper, chilli, spring onions, beansprouts, garlic and ginger for 2 to 3 minutes.

5. Pour in the sauce ingredients and bring to the boil. Cook for 2 minutes until it looks sticky.

6. Add the beef back into the pan and coat in the sticky sauce.

7. Serve with rice or noodles and garnish with sliced spring onions and chillies.

CREAMY HARISSA CHICKEN

PREP TIME: 5 MINUTES | COOKING TIME: 15 MINUTES | SERVES: 2

These spicy chicken cutlets are super quick to make and are perfect all year round. When you're short on time but want delicious food then this one's for you, no matter the season.

INGREDIENTS

80g plain flour

1 tsp paprika

1 tsp garlic powder

2 chicken breasts

1 onion, diced

250ml chicken stock

100g kale, thinly sliced

100g mascarpone

2 tbsp harissa paste

METHOD

1. Place the flour, paprika and garlic powder in a bowl and mix well.

2. Slice the chicken in half lengthways and coat in the seasoned flour.

3. Heat some oil in a large frying pan and cook the chicken cutlets until they are golden-brown on both sides.

4. Remove the chicken from the pan and set aside, then add the onion and cook until it has softened.

5. Pour in the chicken stock and add in the kale. Cook for a couple of minutes.

6. Stir through the mascarpone and the harissa paste, then return the chicken to the pan. Turn down to a medium heat to warm the chicken through.

7. Season to taste then dish it up. This is a versatile dish that will go well with rice, potatoes, or even just a side of veggies.

COD & CHORIZO STEW

PREP TIME: 5 MINUTES | COOKING TIME: 25 MINUTES | SERVES: 4

Chorizo is the key ingredient in this recipe that really brings this homely stew together. Packed full of hearty goodness and flavour, you won't believe this takes less than half an hour to be on the table.

INGREDIENTS

300g baby potatoes, halved

1 onion, diced

1 carrot, diced

2 celery stalks, diced

150g chorizo, cut into chunks

4 cloves of garlic, chopped

1 x 400g tin of chopped tomatoes

400ml vegetable stock

1 x 400g tin of cannellini beans, drained

1 bunch of fresh parsley, chopped

4 cod fillets

METHOD

1. Preheat the oven to 180°c.

2. Parboil the potatoes for 6 to 7 minutes until a knife will cut through them. Drain and set aside.

3. Meanwhile, in a large frying pan, fry the onion, carrot and celery over a medium heat for 5 minutes until the onions have softened.

4. Add the chorizo and cook for a few minutes more until the oil has released.

5. Next, add the chopped garlic, stir well, and cook for a further minute.

6. Pour in the chopped tomatoes, followed by the vegetable stock.

7. Add the cannellini beans and the parboiled potatoes. Season to taste and bring to the boil.

8. Stir through half of the chopped parsley, then transfer the stew to an ovenproof dish.

9. Season the cod fillets with salt and pepper, then lay them over the top, submerging them slightly in the sauce.

10. Bake in the oven for 15 minutes, or until the fish has cooked.

11. Finish with the remaining chopped parsley and serve.

CREAMY TARRAGON CHICKEN

PREP TIME: 5 MINUTES | COOKING TIME: 15 MINUTES | SERVES: 2

Tarragon is a delicious but underused herb that works wonders in this dish. Its distinctly aromatic flavour pairs perfectly with the rich garlicky sauce, creating a fast and fantastic midweek meal.

INGREDIENTS

2 chicken breasts

20g butter

1 onion, diced

3 cloves of garlic, chopped

100ml white wine

150ml chicken stock

150ml double cream

25g tarragon, chopped

METHOD

1. Place the chicken breasts into a sandwich bag and lightly flatten them with a rolling pin. You want the whole breast to be a relatively even width.

2. Season each breast with salt and pepper, then heat some oil and the butter in a frying pan over a medium to high heat.

3. Cook the chicken for 3 to 5 minutes on each side. Once golden, remove the chicken and set aside.

4. Add the diced onion to the pan and cook until it softens, then chuck in the garlic and cook for a further minute.

5. Pour in the white wine and simmer for a minute so that it reduces by half.

6. Add the chicken stock, cream, and tarragon, then return the chicken to the pan. Let it simmer for a few minutes until the sauce starts to thicken.

7. Season to taste and serve. This is a super versatile dish that will pair well with rice, potatoes or even pasta.

GENERAL TSO CHICKEN

PREP TIME: 5 MINUTES | COOKING TIME: 15 MINUTES | SERVES: 2

This is a Chinese dish with a North American twist. It's sweet, savoury, spicy and tangy – perfect for a fakeaway evening dinner.

INGREDIENTS

450g chicken thigh fillets

1 tbsp cornflour

½ tsp garlic powder

½ tsp ground ginger

2 tbsp light sesame oil (untoasted, or any neutral oil)

2 cloves of garlic, chopped

10g ginger, chopped

3 tbsp soy sauce

1 tbsp hoisin sauce

1 tbsp cider vinegar

1 tbsp sriracha

3 tbsp soft brown sugar

TO GARNISH

2 spring onions, sliced

2 tsp sesame seeds

METHOD

1. Cut the chicken thigh fillets into bite-size pieces. Pop them into a bowl and add the cornflour, garlic powder and ground ginger. Toss to coat.

2. Heat the sesame oil in a wok or a large frying pan over a medium to high heat. Add the chicken and cook until it's golden-brown all over.

3. Chuck in the chopped garlic and ginger and stir fry for 1 minute.

4. Add the soy sauce, hoisin, cider vinegar, sriracha and soft brown sugar. Add a splash of water if the sauce needs loosening up slightly.

5. Bring to the boil and cook until the sauce turns sticky.

6. Serve over rice or noodles, then finish with the sliced spring onions and sesame seeds.

HARISSA CHICKEN THIGHS WITH COCONUT RICE

PREP TIME: 5 MINUTES | COOKING TIME: 25 MINUTES | SERVES: 4

When you want something special with no fuss at all, these harissa roasted chicken thighs are the answer. They're spicy, zesty, and delicious and pair perfectly with this coconut-infused rice.

INGREDIENTS

FOR THE CHICKEN

8 skin-on chicken thighs

2 tbsp harissa paste

½ tsp salt

FOR THE COCONUT RICE

300g basmati rice

400ml coconut milk

200ml water

10g fresh coriander

1 lime, zested

METHOD

FOR THE CHICKEN

1. Preheat the oven to 200°c.

2. Pop the chicken thighs into a bowl, then add the harissa paste, salt, and a drizzle of oil. Mix well to completely coat the chicken.

3. Place the thighs onto a baking tray, skin side up, and roast for 25 minutes.

FOR THE COCONUT RICE

1. Tip the rice into a sieve and rinse under cold water until it runs clear to remove the excess starch.

2. Pop the rinsed rice into a large pot, then pour over the coconut milk and the water.

3. Add a pinch of salt and bring to a boil over a high heat, then turn down to a simmer for 10 minutes.

4. Remove from the heat, cover, and leave to stand for 5 more minutes.

5. Fluff up the rice with a fork and stir through the coriander and lime zest. Serve alongside the harissa chicken.

HONEY & MUSTARD CHICKEN

PREP TIME: 5 MINUTES | COOKING TIME: 15 MINUTES | SERVES: 2

This creamy Honey and Mustard Chicken has tender, melt-in-your-mouth chicken breasts and a silky honey mustard sauce. It's quick and easy to make, so it's great for busy weeknights but tasty enough for company!

INGREDIENTS

2 chicken breasts

100g plain flour

2 tbsp neutral oil

20g butter

1 onion, diced

2 cloves of garlic, chopped

100ml chicken stock

2 tbsp honey

2 tbsp wholegrain mustard

150ml double cream

1 small bunch of parsley, chopped

METHOD

1. Cut the chicken breasts in half lengthways to make four thin fillets.
2. Season the flour with salt and pepper, then coat each piece of chicken with it.
3. Heat the oil and butter in a large frying pan over a medium to high heat. Pan fry the chicken until it is golden-brown on both sides. Remove the chicken from the pan and set aside.
4. To make the sauce, turn the heat down to medium, add the diced onion, and cook for about 5 minutes until it starts to soften.
5. Add the garlic and cook for a further minute.
6. Pour in the chicken stock, then add the honey and mustard. Bring to the boil.
7. Pour in the cream and pop the chicken back into the pan. Give it a stir.
8. Cook for a few minutes, stirring occasionally until the sauce thickens.
9. Add the chopped parsley and season to taste. Serve with buttery new potatoes and asparagus, or your choice of potatoes and vegetables.

HONEY GARLIC BAKED SALMON

PREP TIME: 5 MINUTES | COOKING TIME: 15 MINUTES | SERVES: 2

Here's a quick and uncomplicated way to jazz up a couple of salmon fillets. This recipe is perfect for a tasty midweek dinner that's not only fancy but fuss-free.

INGREDIENTS

2 salmon fillets

30g butter, melted

1 tbsp honey

2 cloves of garlic, minced

½ tsp oregano

¼ tsp paprika

¼ tsp salt

¼ tsp black pepper

½ lemon

METHOD

1. Preheat the oven to 200°c.

2. Place the salmon fillets skin side down in a lined baking tray.

3. Mix the melted butter, honey, garlic, oregano, paprika, salt, and pepper together in a small bowl.

4. Spoon the mixture over the salmon fillets to coat them.

5. Thinly slice the lemon, then cut each slice into half-moons. Pop them over and around the salmon.

6. Put the tray into the oven and bake for 12 minutes.

7. Serve with buttery, garlicky new potatoes and tenderstem broccoli.

MARRY ME CHICKEN

PREP TIME: 5 MINUTES | COOKING TIME: 15 MINUTES | SERVES: 2

Legend has it that whomever you cook this dish for will instantly want to marry you. Sadly for some, the real reason behind the name is to do with how well the ingredients marry together. Proposal or not, this creamy chicken dish is super delicious and on the table in minutes.

INGREDIENTS

1 tsp salt

1 tsp black pepper

80g plain flour

2 chicken breasts

20g butter

1 onion, diced

4 cloves of garlic, chopped

200ml chicken stock

150ml double cream

60g parmesan, grated

2 tbsp sundried tomato paste

1 tsp dried thyme

1 tsp dried oregano

1 bunch of fresh basil, roughly chopped

METHOD

1. Add the salt and pepper to the flour and mix well. Coat the chicken in the seasoned flour and shake off any excess.

2. Add a little oil and the butter to a large frying pan on a medium to high heat. Once the butter has melted, add the chicken and cook until it's golden-brown on both sides. This will take about 3 to 4 minutes on each side.

3. Remove the chicken from the pan and set aside. Using the same pan, fry the onion for a few minutes until it starts to soften.

4. Chuck in the garlic and cook for a further minute.

5. Pour in the chicken stock and double cream, then add the grated parmesan. Stir well and turn down to a simmer.

6. Add the sundried tomato paste, thyme, and oregano, and stir well.

7. Return the chicken to the pan and simmer until the sauce has thickened and the chicken has cooked through.

8. Season to taste, top with the fresh basil, and serve with Hasselback potatoes and broccoli, or your choice of potatoes, pasta or rice.

MUSTARD STUFFED CHICKEN

PREP TIME: 5 MINUTES | COOKING TIME: 25 MINUTES | SERVES: 4

Don't let your chicken dinners be boring! This recipe takes no time at all and will leave you feeling like you've just cooked restaurant-quality food at home. Perfect for midweek or even when you're hosting, this one is a real winner.

INGREDIENTS

125g mozzarella, torn into small pieces

80g mature cheddar, grated

1 tbsp wholegrain mustard

4 chicken breasts

12 rashers of streaky bacon

50ml white wine

1 bulb of garlic

3 sprigs of rosemary

3 sprigs of thyme

METHOD

1. Preheat the oven to 200°c.

2. Mix the mozzarella, grated cheddar and wholegrain mustard together.

3. Slice a pocket into the side of each chicken breast and stuff with the mustard and cheese mixture.

4. Wrap each breast with three streaky bacon rashers – not too tightly, but enough to hold it together.

5. Season with salt and pepper and place on a baking tray.

6. Add the white wine, garlic and herbs.

7. Roast for about 25 minutes.

8. Serve with your choice of potatoes, vegetables, or rice.

ONE-POT MEXICAN CHICKEN & RICE

PREP TIME: 10 MINUTES | **COOKING TIME:** 20 MINUTES | **SERVES:** 6

This One-Pot Mexican Chicken & Rice is the easiest dinner. It's made with enchilada sauce and has loads of tasty toppings. There's cheese, avocado, soured cream, tomato, and coriander... so I mean loads!

INGREDIENTS

1 onion, diced

450g chicken breast, cut into bite-size pieces

2 cloves of garlic, chopped

200g long grain rice

340g red enchilada sauce

1 x 400g tin of chopped tomatoes

1 tsp ground cumin

200g cheddar, grated

TO SERVE (OPTIONAL)

100ml soured cream

2 beef tomatoes, diced

1 avocado, diced

10g coriander, roughly chopped

METHOD

1. Heat a little oil in a casserole pot over a medium to high heat. Add the diced onion and cook for a few minutes until it softens.

2. Add the chicken and season with salt and black pepper. Cook for 4 to 5 minutes, stirring occasionally until it starts to brown.

3. Add the garlic and cook for a further minute.

4. Add the rice and stir. Cook for a couple of minutes.

5. Pour in the enchilada sauce, chopped tomatoes, cumin, and 240ml of water. Stir to combine, then bring to the boil. Turn down to a simmer, and cover with a lid or tin foil.

6. Cook for about 12 to 14 minutes, stirring occasionally, until the rice is tender and the liquid has been absorbed.

7. Remove the lid and sprinkle over the grated cheese. Let it sit for two minutes to let the cheese melt.

8. Sprinkle over the remaining toppings and serve.

PORK NOODLE STIR FRY

PREP TIME: 5 MINUTES | COOKING TIME: 10 MINUTES | SERVES: 2

Stir frying is a fast and efficient cooking method that was developed in China, and you can't get much faster and simpler than this Pork Noodle Stir Fry! This recipe is perfect for nights where you want a satisfying meal without spending lots of time or money.

INGREDIENTS

350g minced pork

300g egg noodles

4 cloves of garlic, chopped

5g ginger, chopped

1 red onion, sliced

1 carrot, grated

160g mangetout

2 peppers, sliced

2 tsp cornflour

4 tbsp soy sauce

4 tbsp sweet chilli sauce

METHOD

1. Heat some oil in a wok or a large frying pan over a medium to high heat. Add the minced pork and break it up using a wooden spoon or spatula.

2. Cook the mince for about 8 to 10 minutes, stirring occasionally until it starts to brown and the liquid has evaporated.

3. Meanwhile, prepare the egg noodles as per the packet instructions.

4. Once the mince has browned, add the garlic, ginger, red onion, grated carrot, mangetout, and peppers, and stir fry for a few minutes.

5. To make the sauce, mix the cornflour and soy sauce in a bowl to make a smooth paste. Add the sweet chilli sauce along with a splash of water to help loosen it.

6. Add the sauce and cooked noodles to the pan and stir well until everything is nicely coated.

7. Serve immediately.

PEANUT BUTTER CHICKEN

PREP TIME: 5 MINUTES | COOKING TIME: 15 MINUTES | SERVES: 2

This easy Peanut Butter Chicken recipe is the perfect meal for any day of the week. With only a handful of ingredients, most of which you'll find in the cupboard, and 30 minutes in the kitchen, you can create a wonderful dinner the entire family will enjoy.

INGREDIENTS

1 onion, diced

2 chicken breasts, cut into chunks

2 tsp garlic paste

2 tsp ginger paste

1 tbsp mild curry powder

1 tsp ground cumin

1 x 400ml tin of coconut milk

2 tbsp soy sauce

120g smooth peanut butter

1 tbsp honey

10g coriander, finely chopped

TO SERVE

1 red chilli, finely sliced

A handful of roasted peanuts

METHOD

1. Pan fry the diced onion over a medium to high heat for about 5 minutes until it starts to soften.

2. Add the chicken into the pan and cook until it's sealed and no more pink bits are visible.

3. Add the garlic, ginger, curry powder, and cumin, then give it a stir and cook for a minute to release the flavours.

4. Turn the heat down to medium then pour in the coconut milk and soy sauce.

5. Leave to simmer for 4 to 5 minutes until the chicken is cooked through.

6. Add the peanut butter and honey and stir well.

7. At the last minute, sprinkle in the chopped coriander.

8. Serve with rice and finish with roasted peanuts and sliced chilli.

FIRECRACKER CHICKEN

PREP TIME: 5 MINUTES | COOKING TIME: 15 MINUTES | SERVES: 2

This spicy chicken stir fry is not for the faint-hearted. Did you know that eating chillies releases endorphins, similarly to a runner's high, or like the roller-coaster rides that adrenaline junkies crave? You could say that this dish will make you feel alive! Not bad for under 30 minutes in the kitchen.

INGREDIENTS

2 chicken breasts

2 tbsp cornflour

1 tbsp cayenne pepper

1 red pepper, sliced

1 yellow pepper, sliced

100g mangetout

2 cloves of garlic, chopped

1 red chilli, sliced (or more for extra heat)

3 tbsp soy sauce

2 tbsp sweet chilli sauce

2 tbsp sriracha

2 tbsp tomato ketchup

2 tbsp cider vinegar

4 spring onions, sliced

METHOD

1. Start by slicing the chicken into thin strips. Pop the chicken into a bowl, then add the cornflour and cayenne pepper. Toss to coat.

2. Heat some oil in a large frying pan or wok and cook the chicken over a medium to high heat until it's golden and cooked through.

3. Add the red pepper, yellow pepper and mangetout. Cook for 2 to 3 minutes until softened.

4. Add the garlic and chilli and cook for a further minute.

5. Turn the heat down to medium and add the soy sauce, sweet chilli, sriracha, ketchup and cider vinegar.

6. Bring to the boil, then take off the heat.

7. Serve with rice and finish with a sprinkling of sliced spring onions.

PRAWN, ASPARAGUS & COURGETTE RISOTTO

PREP TIME: 10 MINUTES | COOKING TIME: 15 MINUTES | SERVES: 4

When I was working in the restaurant, this was one of the dishes I came up with. We would cook the base of the risotto then chill it so when it came to service, this tasty dish could be whipped up in less than 8 minutes. You can do this at home, too!

INGREDIENTS

1 litre vegetable stock

1 onion, diced

300g risotto rice

300ml white wine

1 red chilli, sliced

5 cloves of garlic, chopped

1 courgette, diced

100g asparagus, tips separated and ends sliced

200g raw king prawns

200g parmesan, grated

100g unsalted butter

METHOD

1. To make the base, add the vegetable stock to a pan on a medium heat and leave to simmer.

2. Heat a little oil in a large frying pan over a medium to high heat. Fry the onion until it softens, then add the risotto rice. (It's important to toast the rice before adding any liquid, as this enables it to soak up the flavour.)

3. When the rice starts to crackle and pop, add the white wine. It should sizzle and steam.

4. Reduce by half, then start to ladle in the stock, stirring the rice in between.

5. Keep adding the stock bit by bit, stirring continuously and allowing the rice to absorb the liquid each time. Repeat this until the rice is al dente, then turn off the heat. (At this point, you can chill the risotto base and keep it in the fridge for 2 days or freeze it for up to a month!)

6. In a separate pan, heat some oil over a medium heat. Add the chilli and garlic and cook for a minute.

7. Add the courgette, sliced asparagus ends, and prawns. Stir fry for 2 more minutes.

8. Add a ladle of vegetable stock as well as the risotto base, then mix to combine.

9. Once the previous ladleful of stock has been absorbed, add another, stirring continuously. Stirring the rice releases the starch and helps to create the risotto's distinct creamy texture.

10. Once the rice is fully cooked, add the asparagus tips, parmesan, and butter, and stir.

11. Season to taste then serve immediately. Finish with more parmesan, if desired.

SWEET & SOUR CHICKEN

PREP TIME: 5 MINUTES | COOKING TIME: 20 MINUTES | SERVES: 2

This is my homemade Sweet & Sour Chicken with a better-than-takeout sauce. This recipe is Hong Kong style, meaning the chicken is chopped into bite-size pieces, dredged in a flavourful coating, then crisped to perfection before being coated in the sauce.

INGREDIENTS

100g plain flour

1 tbsp paprika

100g cornflour

3 eggs, beaten

500g chicken, diced

1 red onion, cut into large chunks

2 peppers, roughly chopped

1 tbsp garlic paste

1 tbsp ginger paste

150g tomato ketchup

2 tbsp cider vinegar

1 tbsp soy sauce

90g soft brown sugar

1 x 435g tin of pineapple chunks, including the juice

METHOD

1. Tip the plain flour into a tray or a large bowl, then add the paprika as well as a pinch of salt and pepper. Mix well.

2. Add the cornflour into a second tray or bowl, and the eggs into a third.

3. Coat the diced chicken in the cornflour, followed by the beaten egg and finally the seasoned flour.

4. Heat some oil in a large frying pan or a wok, then fry the chicken over a medium to high heat until it's golden and crispy. You might need to do this in batches.

5. Remove the chicken from the pan and place it onto kitchen paper to get rid of any excess oil. Set aside.

6. Wipe the pan clean, then heat some more oil. Fry the onion for 2 to 3 minutes until it softens.

7. Add the peppers and cook for a minute. Then add the garlic and ginger and cook for a further minute.

8. Add the remaining ingredients to the pan to create the sweet and sour sauce.

9. Stir together, then bring to the boil. Once it's boiling, turn down to a simmer and carry on cooking for a few minutes until the sauce has thickened slightly.

10. Add the chicken back into the pan, stir to coat, and warm it through.

11. Serve with rice and a sprinkling of sesame seeds.

PROPER COMFORT FOOD

For many, comfort food is any food that conjures a nostalgic feeling or brings back fond memories of childhood or of a loved one's home cooking. It's often something we turn to when we feel overwhelmed or stressed. Comfort food brings a sense of happiness, warmth and, most of all, comfort.

The dishes we define as comfort food are often a personal choice, but in this chapter, I've compiled some of my favourites for you to enjoy.

THE ULTIMATE MAC & CHEESE

PREP TIME: 15 MINUTES | COOKING TIME: 45 MINUTES | SERVES: 6

Though its exact origins are unknown, the earliest known recipe for macaroni and cheese is from a 1769 book called The Experienced English Housekeeper. The recipe has changed a lot over the years, but here's my ultimate version. What makes it ultimate? The addition of pancetta, spring onions, crunchy bread and LOADS of cheese.

INGREDIENTS

400g macaroni (though any short pasta will do)

240g pancetta lardons

2 cloves of garlic, chopped

1 tsp mustard powder

40g butter

40g plain flour

568ml whole milk (1 pint)

450g mature cheddar, grated

50g parmesan, grated

100g spring onions, sliced

60g baguette, cut into small cubes

½ tsp smoked paprika

METHOD

1. Preheat the oven to 180°c.

2. Add the pasta to salted boiling water and cook for 2 minutes less than the packet instructions. Once cooked, drain in a colander and set aside.

3. Meanwhile, add the pancetta into a cold pan without any oil, and turn the heat to high. The pancetta will cook in its own fat, so cook it for a few minutes until it starts to crisp up.

4. Turn the heat down to medium, then add the garlic and the mustard powder and cook for 30 seconds.

5. Add the butter and, once it has fully melted, add the plain flour and stir it in. Cook for one minute, stirring continuously.

6. Add the milk bit by bit, whisking continuously until you have used up all the milk and there are no lumps in the sauce.

7. Simmer for a few minutes until the sauce has thickened.

8. Take it off the heat and stir in 250g of the grated cheddar and 25g of the grated parmesan. Stir until the cheese has melted fully and season to taste.

9. Stir in the spring onions and drained pasta.

10. Place the cubes of bread into the oven and bake for 3 to 4 minutes to crisp them up slightly.

11. Pour the cheesy pasta into an ovenproof dish, then sprinkle over the remaining cheese. Scatter the toasted cubes of bread over the top and finish with the smoked paprika.

12. Bake in the oven for 20 to 22 minutes until the top is golden and crisp, then serve.

BEEF & GUINNESS STEW WITH DUMPLINGS

PREP TIME: 15 MINUTES | COOKING TIME: 2 HOURS 30 MINUTES | SERVES: 4-6

Classic beef stew with dumplings is perhaps the king of all comfort food. For many people, this will take them back to the cold winter months of their childhood. I like the dumplings to be soft on the bottom and crispy on top.

INGREDIENTS

FOR THE STEW

20g butter

800g braising steak, diced

150g pancetta

1 large onion, diced

4 cloves of garlic, crushed

3 celery stalks, cut into chunks

2 leeks, roughly chopped

2 tbsp plain flour

400ml Guinness

250ml beef stock

3 bay leaves

1 bunch each of fresh rosemary & fresh thyme, finely chopped

3 carrots, peeled and cut into chunks

1 swede, cut into chunks

10 peeled baby onions

2 tbsp Worcestershire sauce

FOR THE DUMPLINGS

150g plain flour

1 tsp baking powder

75g beef suet

½ bunch of rosemary, finely chopped

100ml water

METHOD

1. Preheat the oven to 180°c.

2. Heat 2 tablespoons of sunflower oil and the butter in a large frying pan, then add the beef and fry until browned on all sides.

3. Meanwhile, add the pancetta to an ovenproof casserole pot and cook on a high heat until the pancetta starts to crisp. Add the diced onion, garlic, celery and leeks and cook until the onions are soft.

4. Once the beef has browned, mix in the flour, then add the beef into the casserole pot.

5. Stir in the Guinness, beef stock, herbs, and remaining vegetables.

6. Add the Worcestershire sauce then season well with salt and pepper.

7. Cover the pot with a lid and transfer to the oven and cook for 2 hours, or until the meat is tender.

8. Meanwhile, prepare the dumplings by adding the flour, baking powder, beef suet, some salt, and rosemary into a mixing bowl. Add the water a little at a time until a thick dough forms. You may not need to use all of the water.

9. With floured hands, roll the dough into eight equal-sized balls.

10. After the stew has cooked for 2 hours, remove the lid and place the dumpling balls on top, half submerged in the stew.

11. Return to the oven without the lid for a further 20 minutes, or until the dumplings are puffed up and golden.

WHOLE CURRIED CHICKEN TRAYBAKE

PREP TIME: 10 MINUTES | COOKING TIME: 1 HOUR | SERVES: 4

Let the oven do the hard work for you with this delicious all-in-one chicken traybake. Maximum flavour, minimal effort. What's not to love?

INGREDIENTS

800g baby potatoes, halved

3 peppers, roughly chopped

2 red onions, roughly chopped

4 tbsp mild curry paste

1.4kg whole chicken

10g coriander, chopped

METHOD

1. Preheat the oven to 180°c.

2. Add the potatoes, peppers, and red onion into a 30cm x 40cm roasting tray. Add 2 tablespoons of curry paste and toss to coat.

3. Spatchcock the chicken by first flipping the chicken over so that the breasts are facing down. Use scissors or a sharp knife to carefully cut down either side of the backbone to remove it. Then, flip the chicken back around and press down on top of the breast until it flattens and cracks.

4. Place the spatchcocked chicken on top of the vegetables, skin side up. Rub the remaining curry paste over the chicken and season with salt and pepper.

5. Roast for 1 hour or until cooked through, then sprinkle with the chopped coriander and serve.

BEEF GOULASH

PREP TIME: 20 MINUTES | COOKING TIME: 2 HOURS 30 MINUTES, OR 4-7 HOURS IN SLOW COOKER | SERVES: 6

This classic Hungarian stew is packed with paprika and peppers. You can cook this on the stove, or in your slow cooker. It's a versatile dish that pairs with all kinds of carbs, so be sure to experiment with new combinations each time you make it.

INGREDIENTS

2 tbsp plain flour

1kg diced beef

4 onions, thickly sliced

5 cloves of garlic, chopped

2 tbsp hot smoked paprika

500ml beef stock

1 x 400g tin of chopped tomatoes

2 tbsp tomato paste

4 peppers, cut into chunks

TO SERVE

25g parsley, chopped

100ml soured cream

METHOD

ON THE STOVE

1. Season the flour generously with salt and pepper, then coat the diced beef in the seasoned flour. Heat some oil in a large pan, then cook the beef over a medium to high heat until it's browned all over.

2. Add the onions and cook for 5 minutes or until they start to soften.

3. Chuck in the garlic and cook for a further minute, then add the smoked paprika.

4. Add the beef stock, tin of tomatoes, and tomato paste. Stir well, turn the heat down to a low to medium, then cover with a lid or tin foil. Cook for 90 minutes, stirring occasionally.

5. After 90 minutes, add the peppers and cook for a further hour, or until the beef is tender.

6. Season to taste, then top with the parsley and soured cream. Dish up with your choice of pasta, rice, or potatoes.

IN THE SLOW COOKER

1. Season the flour generously with salt and pepper, then coat the diced beef in the seasoned flour. Heat some oil in a large pan, then cook the beef over a medium to high heat until it's browned all over.

2. Add the onions and cook for 5 minutes or until they start to soften.

3. Chuck in the garlic and cook for a further minute, then transfer everything to your slow cooker.

4. Add the remaining ingredients (apart from the soured cream and parsley) and cook on medium for 4 to 5 hours or on low for 5 to 7 hours.

5. Season to taste, then top with the parsley and soured cream. Dish up with your choice of pasta, rice, or potatoes.

CHICKEN & LEEK PIE

PREP TIME: 20 MINUTES | COOKING TIME: 50 MINUTES | SERVES: 5-6

Pies come in all sorts of different shapes and sizes, but the most traditional one in the UK has a meat filling and is entirely encased in pastry. This chicken and leek pie is, technically speaking, a pot pie, as it only has a pie crust top. Comfort food made easy.

INGREDIENTS

40g butter

1 large onion, diced

1 bunch of thyme, finely chopped

50g plain flour

500ml chicken stock

600g chicken thigh fillets (or breast, if preferred)

350g leek, cut into chunks

2 tsp garlic paste

150g créme fraiche

1 tbsp Dijon mustard

80g spinach leaves

1 bunch of tarragon, finely chopped

320g ready-roll puff pastry

1 egg

A few sprigs of rosemary

METHOD

1. Preheat the oven to 180°c.

2. In a large saucepan, heat 20g of the butter with a teaspoon of oil. Fry the onion and thyme on a medium heat for 7 to 8 minutes until soft.

3. Stir in the plain flour and cook for a further minute.

4. Add the chicken stock and stir well to combine.

5. Cut the chicken into bite-size chunks and add to the saucepan. Bring to the boil, then simmer for 10 minutes until the sauce has thickened.

6. Meanwhile, in a large frying pan, heat the remaining butter with a teaspoon of oil. Fry the leeks over a high heat for 2 to 3 minutes, stirring often so they don't burn.

7. Add the garlic paste and cook for a further minute.

8. Add the leeks to the saucepan, then stir in the créme fraiche and Dijon mustard. Add the spinach leaves and stir well until wilted slightly.

9. Add the tarragon, season to taste, then use a large ladle to transfer the filling into a 24cm pie dish.

10. Use a pastry brush to wet the edges of the pie dish, then cut a few 2cm-wide strips of pastry and line the rim of the dish.

11. Lay the remaining pastry across the top of the pie, pressing down around the edges. Use a sharp knife to cut away any excess pastry.

12. Crimp the edges by using the thumb and forefinger of one hand and the forefinger of the other.

13. Cut two slits in the middle of the pastry to allow steam to escape, then poke two sprigs of rosemary into the slits.

14. Lightly beat the egg and brush it over the pastry once cooked.

15. Place the pie into the oven for about 25 to 30 minutes, or until it has puffed up and is golden on top. When it looks done, it's done!

BEEF BRISKET CHILLI

PREP TIME: 15 MINUTES | COOKING TIME: 4 HOURS 10 MINUTES | SERVES: 8

There aren't many dishes more comforting than a fiery chilli con carne. This recipe uses beef brisket and chipotle chilli to give an amazing texture and wonderfully smoky depth of flavour. I like to describe this one as a proper cowboy chilli.

INGREDIENTS

2 red onions, sliced

5 cloves of garlic, chopped

1 red chilli, chopped

4 bay leaves

3 tsp smoked paprika

3 tsp ground cumin

2 tsp ground coriander

2 tsp oregano

2 tsp chipotle chilli paste

2 tbsp tomato paste

2 x 400g tins of chopped tomatoes

250ml beef stock

1kg trimmed brisket

2 peppers, diced

2 x 400g tins of mixed beans

60g dark chocolate

Soured cream, to serve

METHOD

1. Heat some oil in a large casserole dish over a medium heat, then fry the onions, garlic, and chilli for a few minutes.

2. Add the bay leaves and dry herbs and spices and continue to cook until the onions have softened. If the pan becomes dry from the spices, just add a splash of water.

3. Add the chipotle chilli and tomato paste, stir well, and cook for a further minute.

4. Pour in the tins of chopped tomatoes and beef stock.

5. While the sauce is simmering, dice the brisket into rough 2cm cubes. Drop it straight into the pan and give it a stir to make sure the meat is submerged. Season, then simmer for 3 to 4 hours with the lid on, stirring occasionally to prevent it from sticking.

6. After 3 to 4 hours, once the meat is very tender, remove the bay leaves and use two forks to break up the meat and pull it apart.

7. Add the peppers, tinned beans, and chocolate and warm through.

8. Season to taste, then serve with basmati rice and a dollop of soured cream.

CHILLI HOTPOT

PREP TIME: 15 MINUTES | COOKING TIME: 1 HOUR 20 MINUTES | SERVES: 8

For an unrivalled comforting dish, take chilli con carne to another level by turning it into a hotpot! The crispy sliced potatoes turn this into a completely different dish.

INGREDIENTS

1 large onion, diced

2 tsp ground cumin

1 tsp ground coriander

2 tsp smoked paprika

2 tsp garlic paste

2 tsp chipotle chilli paste

1 x 400g tin of chopped tomatoes

1 tbsp tomato paste

1 beef stock cube

1 tbsp instant coffee

350ml boiling water

750g minced beef

1 x 400g tin of beans (I used kidney beans and butter beans)

1 red pepper, diced

800g Maris Piper potatoes, thinly sliced

60g butter, melted

Pinch of dried oregano

METHOD

1. Preheat the oven to 200°c.

2. Fry the diced onion in a hot saucepan for a few minutes until soft.

3. Add the ground cumin, coriander and smoked paprika. Cook for a couple of minutes, adding a splash of water if it becomes too dry.

4. Add the garlic and chipotle paste, cook for one minute, then add the chopped tomatoes and tomato paste.

5. Add the beef stock cube and the coffee granules to a jug with the boiling water and stir until dissolved.

6. Pour the stock into the saucepan, then turn the heat down to medium and leave to simmer.

7. Meanwhile, add the minced beef into a large frying pan and cook over a high heat. Use a wooden spoon or a spatula to break up the mince until you don't have any chunks left. Cook until the beef has browned and any liquid has evaporated.

8. Add the beef to the sauce, stir well, and leave to simmer for 10 minutes.

9. Add the beans and diced pepper and cook for a further 10 minutes.

10. Season to taste and transfer the chilli to an ovenproof dish.

11. Layer the thinly sliced potatoes on top of the chilli, starting from the outside and moving towards the centre.

12. Brush the potatoes with the melted butter and sprinkle the dried oregano over the top. Bake for 50 minutes, or until the potatoes are golden and crispy.

CHICKEN GUMBO

PREP TIME: 10 MINUTES | COOKING TIME: 20 MINUTES | SERVES: 4

Known as the holy trinity of Southern American cooking, this recipe sautés peppers, celery, and onion with hearty bacon and chicken, before simmering with chicken broth, crushed tomatoes, and punchy Cajun seasoning.

INGREDIENTS

500g chicken thighs, cut into chunks

150g bacon lardons

1 onion, diced

2 cloves of garlic, chopped

2 celery stalks, finely diced

2 green peppers, diced

1 bay leaf

2 tbsp plain flour

1 tbsp Cajun seasoning

1 x 400g tin of chopped tomatoes

250ml chicken stock

2 tbsp chopped fresh sage

METHOD

1. Heat some oil in a large pan, then add the chicken and cook for 5 minutes until browned. Remove from the pan and set aside.

2. Add the bacon to the same pan and cook for 2 to 3 minutes until it starts to crisp.

3. Add the onion, garlic, celery, green pepper, and bay leaf to the pan and cook for 5 minutes.

4. Return the chicken to the pan, then stir in the flour and Cajun seasoning and cook for 30 seconds.

5. Pour in the tin of tomatoes and the stock, then add the chopped sage and stir to combine. Bring to the boil, then turn down to a simmer, cover, and cook for 10 minutes.

6. Remove the lid, stir well, and cook for another 5 minutes.

7. Season to taste and serve with crusty bread.

LAMB & CHICKPEA CURRY

PREP TIME: 10 MINUTES | COOKING TIME: 2 HOURS 20 MINUTES, OR 4-8 HOURS IN A SLOW COOKER | SERVES: 4

This curry breaks some of the 'rules', but that's ok. When you want delicious food in the simplest way, this is the dish for you. I've even explained how to make this in the slow cooker too, meaning you can just bung everything in and leave it all day.

INGREDIENTS

1 onion, diced

4 cloves of garlic, chopped

1 red chilli, chopped

10g ginger, chopped

1 tbsp curry powder

1 tbsp ground cumin

1 tsp ground coriander

½ tsp ground cinnamon

1 tbsp tomato paste

1 x 400g tin of chopped tomatoes

1 x 400g tin of coconut milk

600g lamb shoulder, diced

2 x 400g tins of chickpeas, drained

1 bunch of coriander, finely chopped

METHOD

1. Fry the onion over a medium to high heat for about 5 minutes until it softens.

2. Chuck in the garlic, chilli and ginger. Cook for a further minute.

3. Add the curry powder, cumin, coriander, cinnamon, and tomato paste. Stir well and cook for 2 more minutes.

4. Pour in the chopped tomatoes and coconut milk, then add the lamb shoulder. Stir well, cover with a lid and leave to simmer over a low to medium heat for about 2 hours, or until the meat is tender.

5. Add the drained chickpeas and cook for a further 20 minutes.

6. Season to taste, then stir through the chopped coriander. Dish it up with basmati rice and enjoy.

SLOW COOKER METHOD

1. Follow the first two steps above, then transfer the onion mixture to your slow cooker along with the rest of the ingredients except the chickpeas and fresh coriander.

2. Cook on low for 8 hours or high for 4 hours. Add the chickpeas for the last hour.

3. Stir through the chopped coriander and taste to check the seasoning once done.

DID YOU KNOW...?

ONIONS COUNT TOWARDS YOUR 5-A-DAY

When adding diced onions to your dishes, you might not think they count towards your 5-a-day, but they're a vegetable as well as a flavour enhancer!

They're also low in calories and high in fibre.

LAMB MOUSSAKA

PREP TIME: 25 MINUTES | COOKING TIME: 1 HOUR 15 MINUTES | SERVES: 6

In its basic form, moussaka consists of layers of aubergine and minced lamb or beef, topped with an enriched béchamel sauce and baked. It's traditionally a Middle Eastern dish, but Greece and Bulgaria also have their own versions.

INGREDIENTS

800g minced lamb

1 onion, diced

2 tsp garlic paste

2 tbsp oregano

1 tbsp dried mint

1 tsp paprika

½ tsp ground cinnamon

3 bay leaves

150ml red wine

2 tbsp plain flour

1 x 400g tin of chopped tomatoes

2 tbsp tomato paste

4 medium sized aubergines

800g potatoes (such as Maris Piper or King Edward)

80g parmesan, grated

FOR THE BÉCHAMEL SAUCE

40g butter

40g plain flour

400ml whole milk

40g parmesan, grated

½ tsp ground nutmeg

1 egg

METHOD

1. Heat a splash of oil in a heavy-bottomed pan and add the minced lamb. Use a spatula or a wooden spoon to break up the meat. Brown the lamb, then add the diced onion. Cook for 1 minute before adding the garlic, oregano, mint, paprika, cinnamon and bay leaves. Cook over a medium heat for 10 minutes.

2. Pour in the red wine, then carry on cooking until it has reduced by half. Stir in the flour, then add the tin of tomatoes and tomato paste. Mix well, then leave to simmer on a low heat for at least 30 minutes. If it gets too dry, add a splash of water.

3. Meanwhile, prepare the aubergines and potatoes. Thinly slice the potatoes to about 2mm thick, drop them into salted boiling water, and cook for about 3 to 4 minutes to soften. Drain them in a colander and leave to steam dry. Slice the aubergine slightly thicker than the potatoes. Heat a good amount of oil in a large frying pan and fry the slices of aubergine until browned on both sides. You will need to do this in batches. Place them onto kitchen paper once done.

4. To make the béchamel sauce, melt the butter over a medium to high heat. Add the flour, mix well, and cook for 1 minute to form a roux. Pour the milk in bit by bit, whisking continuously, until all the milk has been used. Keep cooking until the sauce thickens but be careful not to burn it. Take it off the heat and stir in the grated parmesan and the nutmeg, then set aside to cool.

5. Now, preheat the oven to 180°c. Taste the lamb mince for seasoning.

6. To assemble the dish, layer a third of the lamb into a large ovenproof dish. Form a second layer with the sliced potatoes and aubergine. Repeat these layers twice more until you have three layers of mince and vegetables, finishing with the sliced potatoes and aubergines.

7. Add the egg into the cooled béchamel sauce and beat until combined.

8. Pour it over the moussaka until you have a thick, even layer, then sprinkle with the remaining parmesan cheese.

9. Bake for 35 to 45 minutes until deep golden-brown and bubbling. Leave to rest for a few minutes before serving.

CHICKEN, BACON & LEEK COTTAGE PIE

PREP TIME: 15 MINUTES | COOKING TIME: 45 MINUTES | SERVES: 6

This is a twist on a quick and simple family dinner. Hearty cottage pie but packed with chicken, crispy bacon, and leek and topped with cheesy mashed potatoes.

INGREDIENTS

FOR THE PIE FILLING

500g chicken thigh fillets, chopped into bite-size chunks

150g bacon lardons

2 leeks, sliced

1 tbsp plain flour

350ml chicken stock

3 tbsp crème fraiche

100g frozen peas

FOR THE MASHED POTATO TOPPING

1kg Maris Piper potatoes

50g butter

1 tsp ground nutmeg

200ml milk

300g cheddar, grated

METHOD

1. Preheat the oven to 180°c.

2. Heat a little oil in a large frying pan, then add the chicken and bacon lardons and cook over a medium to high heat until golden all over.

3. Add the leeks and cook for another 2 to 3 minutes, or until they have softened.

4. Add the plain flour and stir well.

5. Pour in the chicken stock and cook for 5 minutes, stirring occasionally.

6. Add the crème fraiche and frozen peas and stir well. Season to taste and continue to cook until the sauce thickens, then spoon the mixture into an ovenproof casserole dish.

7. Meanwhile, make the mashed potato topping. Peel and chop the potatoes and pop them into salted water. Bring to the boil and cook until tender.

8. Drain the potatoes and leave them to steam dry. Then, pop them back into the saucepan along with the butter, nutmeg, milk and half of the grated cheddar. Mash until smooth and season to taste.

9. Spread the mash over the top of the pie filling, then sprinkle over the remaining cheese. Bake for 20 minutes or until golden on top.

SAUSAGE CASSEROLE

PREP TIME: 10 MINUTES | COOKING TIME: 30 MINUTES | SERVES: 4

Good, hearty comfort food. Nothing else to say!

INGREDIENTS

8 good-quality sausages

1 red onion, diced

150g chorizo, roughly chopped

100g carrot, diced

100g swede, diced

5 cloves of garlic, chopped

1 tsp paprika

1 tsp oregano

1 red pepper, roughly chopped

150ml red wine (optional)

1 x 400g tin of chopped tomatoes

2 tbsp tomato paste

200ml vegetable stock

150g kale, stalks removed

1 x 400g tin of beans (I used cannellini)

METHOD

1. Heat a little oil in a large casserole pan and fry the sausages over a medium heat until they are nicely browned all over.

2. Once browned, remove the sausages from the pan and set them aside.

3. In the same pan, add the diced red onion and cook for 1 minute.

4. Add the chorizo, carrot and swede and cook for a few minutes, stirring occasionally.

5. Add the garlic, paprika, oregano and red pepper and cook for 1 minute.

6. Pour in the red wine and let it bubble away until it has reduced by half.

7. Add the tin of chopped tomatoes, tomato paste, vegetable stock, and sausages to the pan.

8. Bring to the boil and then turn down to a simmer. Cover with a lid or tin foil, then cook for 10 to 12 minutes.

9. Add the kale and the beans, stir together and cook for a further 5 minutes. There's no need for the lid this time.

10. Season to taste and serve.

BUTTER CHICKEN

PREP TIME: 15 MINUTES, PLUS 30 MINUTES MARINATING | COOKING TIME: 35 MINUTES | SERVES: 2

This is my simple method for making the most amazing butter chicken. Give it a try and you'll soon see why this curry is a popular dish all over the world.

INGREDIENTS

FOR THE MARINATED CHICKEN

400g chicken thigh fillets, cut into bite-size chunks

1 tbsp yoghurt

1 tsp garlic paste

1 tsp ginger paste

2 tsp garam masala

1 tsp turmeric

1 tsp ground cumin

FOR THE SAUCE

50g butter

1 onion, diced

1 tsp garlic paste

1 tsp ginger paste

1 tbsp garam masala

1 tsp ground cumin

1 tsp turmeric

1 tsp paprika

1 tsp chilli powder

1 x 400g tin of chopped tomatoes

150ml double cream

1 tbsp soft brown sugar

10g coriander, finely chopped

METHOD

1. Place the chicken into a bowl and add all the marinade ingredients. Mix well and place in the fridge for at least 30 minutes before cooking. Leave in the fridge overnight for greater depth of flavour.

2. For the sauce, heat a little bit of oil in a large pan over a medium to high heat, then add the butter. Once the butter starts to brown, add the onion and cook until it softens. Be careful not to burn the butter as it will develop a bitter rather than nutty taste.

3. Add the garlic and ginger and cook for 30 seconds, then add the garam masala, cumin, turmeric, paprika, and chilli powder. Fry for 1 minute to release the flavours, adding a splash of water if it gets too dry.

4. Pour in the chopped tomatoes, then use a stick blender to blitz the sauce until smooth.

5. Add the chicken into the pan along with any marinade juices. Stir well, then simmer for 15 minutes.

6. Add the double cream and soft brown sugar, then let it cook for a further 10 minutes until the sauce is thick and bubbling.

7. Season to taste, then finish with the finely chopped coriander. Serve with basmati rice and naan breads.

POSH BANGERS & MASH WITH CARAMELISED ONIONS

PREP TIME: 10 MINUTES | COOKING TIME: 50 MINUTES | SERVES: 4

You'll be surprised by how great this tastes considering there's only a few ingredients involved. When it comes to which wine to use, I always recommend using any wine you'd be happy to drink the leftovers of!

INGREDIENTS

8 Cumberland sausages

2 onions, sliced

350ml red wine

25g butter

4 cloves of garlic, chopped

400g chestnut mushrooms, halved

1 bunch of thyme, chopped

½ bunch of rosemary, chopped

25g plain flour

150ml chicken or vegetable stock

METHOD

1. Preheat the oven to 180°c.
2. Add a little oil to a large casserole dish and cook the sausages over a medium heat until they are browned all over.
3. Remove the sausages from the pan and set them aside.
4. In the same pan, add the sliced onions and cook for 5 minutes. Once they have softened, pour in 100ml of the red wine, then cook for another 10 minutes until the wine has evaporated and the onions have caramelised.
5. Add the butter and, once it's melted, chuck in the garlic, mushrooms, thyme, and rosemary. Cook for about 4 to 5 minutes until the mushrooms have softened.
6. Sprinkle in the flour, then cook for a minute before pouring in the rest of the wine and the chicken or vegetable stock.
7. Stir well, then return the sausages to the pot. Pop the lid on and put in the oven for 30 minutes, removing the lid for the last 10 minutes.
8. Season to taste, then dish it up with creamy mashed potatoes.

BEEF & POTATO CURRY

PREP TIME: 10 MINUTES | COOKING TIME: 2 HOURS 45 MINUTES OR 4-8 HOURS IN SLOW COOKER | SERVES: 6

This Indian-inspired recipe is a rich and delicious dish that will warm you from the inside out. You'll notice there are two methods included in this recipe, as it can be easily adapted for your slow cooker. It's the perfect dish to leave cooking all day and come home to at night!

INGREDIENTS

1 onion, diced

4 cloves of garlic, chopped

10g ginger, chopped

1 red chilli, chopped

1 tbsp curry powder

1 tbsp ground cumin

1 tsp ground coriander

½ tsp ground cinnamon

1 x 400g tin of chopped tomatoes

1 x 400ml tin of coconut milk

1 tbsp tomato paste

600g diced beef (I used ribeye)

400g baby potatoes, quartered

1 bunch of coriander, finely chopped

METHOD

ON THE STOVE

1. In a large saucepan, fry the onion over a medium to high heat for 5 minutes until softened.

2. Chuck in the garlic, ginger, and chilli. Cook for a further minute.

3. Add the curry powder, cumin, coriander, and cinnamon.

4. Add the chopped tomatoes, coconut milk, and tomato paste.

5. Add the diced beef, stir well, then cover with a lid and leave to simmer over a low to medium heat for about 2 hours, or until the beef is tender.

6. Add the potatoes and cook for a further 30 minutes.

7. Season to taste, then add the chopped coriander and serve alongside basmati rice.

IN THE SLOW COOKER

1. Fry the onion over a medium to high heat for 5 minutes until softened.

2. Chuck in the garlic, ginger, and chilli. Cook for a further minute.

3. Add to the slow cooker along with the rest of the ingredients (except the fresh coriander.)

4. Cook on low for 8 hours or on high for 4 hours. Stir through the chopped coriander and season to taste before serving alongside basmati rice.

FISH PIE

Always a favourite with kids and adults alike. A comforting fish pie is such a warming dish, and it's full of the good stuff. The best part is, it's super simple to make and can be ready fairly quickly.

INGREDIENTS

FOR THE MASHED POTATO TOPPING

1kg potatoes

50ml milk

50g butter

200g crème fraiche

100g cheddar, grated

FOR THE PIE FILLING

25g butter

25g plain flour

450ml milk

125g cheddar, grated

400g mixed fish (such as a fish pie mix)

1 tsp Dijon mustard

100g spring onions

165g tinned sweetcorn, drained

100g peas

1 bunch of fresh parsley, chopped

METHOD

1. Preheat the oven to 180°c.

2. Peel the potatoes and chop them into halves and quarters so they're roughly the same size, then put them into a pan of salted water.

3. Bring to the boil, then simmer until the potatoes are tender. Drain them in a colander and leave to steam dry.

4. Mash the potatoes, then stir in the milk, butter and crème fraiche. Season with salt and pepper, then set aside while you prepare the pie filling.

5. Melt the butter in a large saucepan, then add the flour and cook for a further minute.

6. Gradually pour in the milk, whisking continuously over a medium heat to remove any lumps.

7. Once all the milk has been added, continue to cook until the sauce has thickened.

8. Take it off the heat and stir in the grated cheese until it has melted.

9. Add the mixed fish, Dijon mustard, spring onions, sweetcorn, peas and chopped parsley. Stir until well combined.

10. Transfer the mixture into a pie dish, then dollop over the mashed potato and use a fork to rough it up on top.

11. Scatter the remaining cheddar over the top, then bake in the oven for 25 minutes until golden and bubbling at the edges.

PLENTY OF PASTA

I'm often asked what my favourite thing to cook is and, truth be told, it's an impossible question to answer. If I had to choose, then I would say pasta is my favourite – mainly because it's so versatile. The shapes and sizes of pasta, and the endless sauces that can be created for it, make it such an amazing thing. In a modern world where time is of the essence, pasta is also one of the quicker dishes to make, as well as being delicious and filling.

Always cook the pasta in salted boiling water and use the pasta water in your sauces. The pasta releases starch into the water, so when it's added to your sauces, it'll thicken it and help it stick to the pasta, giving it a slick and glossy shine. Plus, if your pasta water is salted, it'll also season the sauce for you.

You may notice that the pasta recipes call for you to cook the pasta for two minutes less than the packet states. This is so the pasta is al dente. In cooking, al dente describes pasta that is cooked to be firm to the bite. In Italian, it means 'to the tooth'.

EASY FOCACCIA

PREP TIME: 20 MINUTES, PLUS 1 HOUR 30 MINUTES FOR PROVING | COOKING TIME: 20 MINUTES | SERVES: 12

This focaccia recipe is the perfect accompaniment to the pasta dishes in this book and also means a lot to me, so I couldn't write a recipe book without including it. Back in 2010 when I first started working in a restaurant, I was tasked with making the bread and pasta daily. Renowned chef Gennaro Contaldo, Jamie Oliver's Italian mentor, would come into the restaurant and teach me how to make the focaccia. If you know him, you won't be surprised to hear about his passion for the ingredients and the love he'd put into making the famous dimpled bread. He often described the dough as a baby and said it should be treated as such.

Making focaccia was one of the very first things in my life that I was praised for. It's where my first taste of success came from, and that's why I hold it dearly in my heart.

This is my easy-to-make version of a classic focaccia, with lots of extra virgin olive oil, garlic and rosemary. Try dipping it in balsamic vinegar and olive oil.

INGREDIENTS

500g strong white bread flour

7g sachet of fast action yeast

120ml extra virgin olive oil

350ml tepid water

6 cloves of garlic, finely chopped

1 bunch of fresh rosemary

Sea salt

METHOD

1. Add the flour and yeast to a large mixing bowl and use a wooden spoon to combine. Add 1 teaspoon of salt.

2. Make a well in the middle, then add 3 tablespoons of the olive oil and half of the water. Mix well, then gradually add the remaining water.

3. Mix it as much as you can with the wooden spoon before tipping it out onto a clean and floured surface.

4. Knead the dough for 5 to 10 minutes until it's soft and not sticky.

5. Grease and line a 20 x 30cm baking tin with baking paper. Place the dough onto it, cover it with cling film, and leave it to prove in a warm place for about 45 minutes or until it has doubled in size.

6. Once it has doubled, press and stretch the dough into the edges of the tin. Drizzle with plenty of olive oil and scatter the chopped garlic and rosemary over the top. Use your fingers to press dimples all over the dough. Season generously with sea salt.

7. Cover with cling film once again and leave in a warm place for about 45 minutes or until it has doubled in size once again.

8. Meanwhile, preheat the oven to 200°c.

9. Bake the focaccia for 20 minutes until it's golden, then remove it from the oven and drizzle more olive oil over the top.

10. Leave to cool slightly before cutting into portions. Serve with extra virgin olive oil and balsamic vinegar.

CHICKEN ALFREDO

PREP TIME: 10 MINUTES | COOKING TIME: 15 MINUTES | SERVES: 2

Alfredo is a popular pasta dish in America but is frowned upon in Italy. I really love and respect the passion that Italians have for their food and culture, but I think they're missing out on this one. Creamy tagliatelle with chicken and parmesan is a marriage made in heaven.

INGREDIENTS

250g pasta (I used tagliatelle)

2 chicken breasts

2 tsp paprika

1 tsp garlic granules

½ tsp salt

½ tsp pepper

2 tbsp cooking oil

20g butter

1 onion, diced

4 cloves of garlic, chopped

150ml chicken stock

300ml double cream

80g parmesan, grated

1 bunch of parsley, chopped

METHOD

1. Cook the pasta in salted boiling water for 2 minutes less than the packet states.

2. Meanwhile, slice the chicken breasts in half lengthways so you have four thinner fillets. Place the chicken into a bowl and add the paprika, garlic granules, salt, and pepper. Drizzle in some oil and mix until the chicken is completely coated.

3. Heat the oil and butter in a large frying pan over a medium to high heat. When the butter starts to brown, fry the chicken for 3 to 4 minutes on each side. Once cooked, remove the chicken from the pan and set it aside. Cut into strips once cool enough to handle.

4. In the same pan, fry the onion for a few minutes until it starts to soften. Add the garlic and cook for a further minute.

5. Now pour in the chicken stock, let it bubble away for a minute and then pour in the double cream.

6. Add the parmesan, give it a stir and then add the chicken back to the pan. Leave it to simmer so that the cream thickens slightly.

7. Drain the pasta, retaining the cooking water, and add the pasta to the sauce along with some of the cooking water. Mix well to combine.

8. Stir in the chopped parsley and taste to check the seasoning. Dish it up and finish with more grated parmesan on top.

BUCATINI AMATRICIANA

PREP TIME: 10 MINUTES | COOKING TIME: 12 MINUTES | SERVES: 2

Amatriciana is a traditional Italian pasta dish typically made using guanciale (an Italian cured meat), tomatoes and pecorino. It's often served with bucatini, which is a spaghetti-like pasta with a hole in the middle, though any long pasta will do. My version of amatriciana uses just a few ingredients to create a delicious and warming tomato-based pasta.

INGREDIENTS

200g bucatini (or any other long pasta)

240g bacon lardons

1 red onion, diced

1 small red pepper, diced

2 cloves of garlic, chopped

100ml red wine

1 x 400g tin of chopped tomatoes

Pecorino, to serve

METHOD

1. Cook the pasta in salted boiling water for 2 minutes less than the packet states.

2. Meanwhile, heat 1 teaspoon of oil in a large frying pan over a medium to high heat. Add the bacon lardons and cook until they start to turn crispy. Season with black pepper.

3. Add the diced red onion and red pepper and cook for a few minutes until they start to soften.

4. Add the chopped garlic and cook for 30 seconds to release the flavours.

5. Pour in the red wine and reduce by half, then add the tinned tomatoes.

6. Stir well and leave to simmer over a medium heat for a couple of minutes.

7. Add the cooked pasta to the sauce along with a little bit of pasta water to loosen up the sauce. Toss together to fully coat the pasta, then season to taste.

8. Dish it up and finish with the grated pecorino.

CHICKEN PESTO PASTA BAKE

PREP TIME: 10 MINUTES | COOKING TIME: 30 MINUTES | SERVES: 4

Sure to be a family favourite (and a great way to sneak in some veggies), this is a recipe you're going to love.

INGREDIENTS

300g fusilli

1 onion, diced

2 chicken breasts, diced

1 small head of broccoli, cut into florets

4 cloves of garlic, chopped

200ml chicken stock

150g basil pesto

150ml crème fraiche

100g tinned sweetcorn, drained

200g cheddar, grated

METHOD

1. Preheat the oven to 180°c.
2. Cook the fusilli in salted boiling water for 4 minutes less than the packet states.
3. Meanwhile, add some oil to a large frying pan and fry the diced onion for about 4 to 5 minutes until softened.
4. Add the diced chicken and cook until it's sealed and there are no more visible pink bits.
5. Chuck in the broccoli and garlic and cook for a further minute, then pour in the chicken stock and simmer for a couple of minutes.
6. Add in the basil pesto, crème fraiche and sweetcorn, and stir it through.
7. Drain the pasta, add it to the sauce, and stir well. Add a little pasta water if the sauce needs loosening up.
8. Transfer the pasta to an ovenproof dish, sprinkle over the grated cheddar, and bake for 20 minutes or until golden on top.

CHORIZO CARBONARA

PREP TIME: 5 MINUTES | COOKING TIME: 15 MINUTES | SERVES: 2

Some people say you'd be jailed in Italy for making this, but this spicy twist on the Italian classic is an absolute winner. It perfectly merges the flavours of Spain and Italy to create a dish that's sure to become a go-to.

INGREDIENTS

240g spaghetti (or any other pasta)

100g parmesan, grated

1 medium egg

2 egg yolks

1 tsp black pepper

150g chorizo, diced

½ onion, diced

2 cloves of garlic, chopped

10g parsley, chopped

METHOD

1. Cook the pasta in salted boiling water for 2 minutes less than the packet states. Reserve some of the pasta water.

2. In a small bowl, add the parmesan, egg, egg yolks and black pepper. Use a fork to beat it together to form a paste.

3. In a large frying pan, cook the chorizo and onion over a medium to high heat for about 5 minutes, or until the onion softens and the chorizo starts to crisp.

4. Chuck in the garlic and cook for another minute.

5. Add a ladle of pasta water and turn off the heat.

6. Add the cooked spaghetti into the pan and toss it through the chorizo and onions, then add in the cheese and egg mixture.

7. Stir well with a pair of tongs to create a creamy sauce. If it needs loosening up, then add some more pasta water.

8. Season to taste, then stir through the chopped parsley. Dish it up and serve with more grated parmesan.

CREAMY LEMON CHICKEN PASTA

PREP TIME: 10 MINUTES | COOKING TIME: 15 MINUTES | SERVES: 2

This is one of my go-to dishes when I want something special but only have a few ingredients and limited time. Ready in under 25 minutes, this creamy, lemony pasta is a winner every time.

INGREDIENTS

200g spaghetti

20g butter

350g chicken breast, cut into bite-size pieces

1 onion, finely diced

4 cloves of garlic, finely chopped

75ml white wine

200g cream cheese

10g parsley, chopped

1 lemon, zested and juiced

30g parmesan, grated, plus extra for serving

METHOD

1. Cook the pasta in salted boiling water for 2 minutes less than the packet states.

2. Meanwhile, heat some oil in a large frying pan over a medium to high heat. Add the butter and, once melted, add the chicken breast and cook for 3 to 4 minutes until slightly golden.

3. Add the diced onion and garlic and cook until the onion starts to soften, and the chicken is almost cooked through.

4. Pour in the wine and reduce by half.

5. Add the cream cheese and stir well. Once the pasta has cooked, add it to the pan along with a little bit of pasta water. Cook for a further minute, stirring to combine.

6. Add the chopped parsley, zest and juice of the lemon and the grated parmesan. Stir well, then season to taste.

7. Top with more grated parmesan and serve.

CREAMY SALMON PASTA

PREP TIME: 10 MINUTES | COOKING TIME: 20 MINUTES | SERVES: 2

This Creamy Salmon Pasta is a simple yet impressive dish. Roasted salmon, spinach and capers are tossed with pasta and a creamy white wine sauce to create the perfect date night meal.

INGREDIENTS

2 salmon fillets

200g spaghetti

40g butter

4 cloves of garlic, chopped

120ml white wine

200g cherry tomatoes, cut into quarters

300ml double cream

2 lemons

200g baby spinach

20g capers

METHOD

1. Preheat the oven to 200°c.

2. Line a baking tray with baking paper and place the salmon skin side down. Season with salt and pepper then bake for 10 to 12 minutes.

3. Meanwhile, cook the pasta in salted boiling water for 2 minutes less than the packet states.

4. Heat the butter in a large frying pan over a medium heat. Add the garlic and cook for a minute, stirring occasionally.

5. Pour in the white wine and reduce by half, then add the cherry tomatoes.

6. Add the double cream and the zest of one lemon. Bring to the boil and cook for a few minutes until the sauce starts to thicken.

7. Drain the pasta, reserving some pasta water. Add the pasta, spinach and capers to the sauce, cooking for about 1 to 2 minutes until the spinach has wilted.

8. Remove the salmon from the oven and slide a spatula between the skin and the flesh to remove the skin. Break the salmon into chunks and add to the pasta sauce.

9. Stir through the juice of half a lemon and season to taste. Add some pasta water if the sauce needs loosening up.

10. Serve immediately with more lemon zest to garnish.

CREAMY SAUSAGE PASTA

PREP TIME: 10 MINUTES | COOKING TIME: 15 MINUTES | SERVES: 2

This dish is perfect for when you're running low on time. Super quick to make but packed full of flavour.

INGREDIENTS

240g penne

1 onion, diced

450g good-quality sausages, skins removed

150g mushrooms, sliced

4 cloves of garlic, chopped

1 tsp oregano

150ml chicken or vegetable stock

100g baby spinach

200ml double cream

80g parmesan, grated

METHOD

1. Cook the pasta in salted boiling water for 2 minutes less than the packet states.

2. Meanwhile, add oil to a large frying pan and cook the onion over a medium to high heat until softened.

3. Add in the sausages (skin removed) and use a spatula or wooden spoon to break them up into small chunks.

4. Add the mushrooms and cook until the sausage meat has cooked, and the mushrooms have softened.

5. Chuck in the garlic and oregano and cook for another minute.

6. Pour in the chicken or vegetable stock and add the spinach. Once the spinach has wilted, pour in the double cream and add the parmesan.

7. Bring to the boil, then turn down to a simmer for 2 to 3 minutes or until the sauce has thickened slightly.

8. Add the penne, toss it together and season to taste. Add some pasta water if it needs loosening up.

9. Dish it up and serve with extra grated parmesan, if you'd like.

LAMB RAGÙ

PREP TIME: 15 MINUTES | COOKING TIME: 3 HOURS, OR 3-8 HOURS IN A SLOW COOKER | SERVES: 6

The term ragù originates from the French ragoût, which is in turn derived from ragouter, meaning 'to awaken the appetite'. In Italian cuisine, ragù is considered a meat-based sauce that is commonly served with pasta. This rich lamb ragù pairs perfectly with pappardelle pasta (think tagliatelle, but bigger), as well as my crunchy pangrattato (see page 142).

INGREDIENTS

FOR THE RAGÙ

700g lamb shoulder, diced into 1-inch pieces with excess fat trimmed

2 medium carrots, diced

1 onion, diced

1 celery stalk, diced

6 cloves of garlic, finely chopped

3 bay leaves

2 sprigs of fresh rosemary

2 tbsp tomato paste

200ml red wine (such as Chianti)

250ml lamb or beef stock

2 x 400g tins of chopped tomatoes

TO SERVE

600g pappardelle

Parmesan, grated

METHOD

1. Season the diced lamb with salt and black pepper. Add 2 tablespoons of oil to a heavy-bottomed pot over a medium to high heat and cook the seasoned lamb until deeply browned all over, working in batches to avoid overcrowding the pot. Transfer the lamb to a plate and set aside.

2. Add a little more oil to the pan, reduce the heat to medium, then add the diced carrot, onion and celery. Cook, stirring occasionally, until the veggies are softened. This will take about 10 to 15 minutes.

3. Stir in the garlic, bay leaves and rosemary and cook for 1 minute more, then add the tomato paste and stir to coat the veggies. Cook for 1 to 2 minutes to caramelise the tomato paste.

4. Pour in the red wine and use a wooden spoon to scrape up any brown bits that have formed in the bottom of the pan – it's all flavour. Let the wine reduce by half, then pour in the stock and tinned tomatoes.

5. Pop the lamb back into the pan and stir well. At this point you have three options for cooking the ragù:

IN A CASSEROLE POT

Preheat the oven to 165°c. Place the lid on the casserole pot and put it into the oven to braise for 2 hours and 30 minutes.

ON THE STOVE

Cover the pan with either tin foil or a lid and cook over a medium heat for 2 hours and 30 minutes, stirring occasionally to make sure it's not sticking.

IN THE SLOW COOKER

Place all the ingredients into a slow cooker and cook on high for 3 hours or on low for 8 hours.

TO SERVE

1. When it's ready, the lamb should fall apart very easily. It should be tender enough to shred into the ragù with a wooden spoon. Remove the sprigs of rosemary and bay leaves, and season to taste.

2. You can now serve the ragù, chill it, or chill then freeze it. It will keep in the fridge for up to 3 days or the freezer for up to 3 months.

3. When you're ready to serve the ragù, boil the pasta in salted boiling water for 2 minutes less than the packet states. Drain it but keep some of the pasta water. Toss the pasta with the ragù and add a little pasta water to loosen up. Dish it up and serve with lots of grated parmesan.

DID YOU KNOW...?

SALT WAS USED AS CURRENCY

The word 'salary' is derived from the word 'salt.' In ancient times, salt was highly valued, and its production was legally restricted, so it was used as a method of trade and currency.

Salt is still used for trade among the nomads of Ethiopia's Danakil Plains.

LAND & SEA LINGUINE

PREP TIME: 10 MINUTES | COOKING TIME: 20 MINUTES | SERVES: 2

This is a special dish that is sure to wow you. Using ingredients from both land and sea, this one is simply bursting with flavour.

INGREDIENTS

200g linguine

75g sausage (approx. 1 sausage), skin removed

75g pancetta

75g mushrooms, cut into quarters

4 cloves of garlic, chopped

1 red chilli, chopped

80ml white wine

100ml chicken stock

75g raw king prawns, peeled

75g white fish, such as cod, diced

20g butter

40g crème fraiche

15g parsley, chopped

½ lemon, juiced

METHOD

1. Cook the pasta in salted boiling water for 2 minutes less than the packet states.

2. In a large frying pan, over a medium to high heat, add the sausage (skin removed) and the pancetta. You don't need to add oil as the pancetta will release fat. Use a wooden spoon to break up the sausage meat.

3. Cook until the pancetta starts to crisp up and the sausage meat has browned. Add the mushrooms and cook for a further 2 minutes.

4. Chuck in the garlic and chilli and cook for 1 minute before pouring in the white wine. Let it reduce by half, then pour in the chicken stock.

5. Add the prawns and the white fish, then turn down to a simmer for a couple of minutes until the fish cooks through.

6. Add the pasta and a little bit of the pasta water. Then, stir through the butter, crème fraiche, parsley, and the juice of half a lemon. Season to taste and serve.

MUSHROOM & BACON FETTUCCINE

PREP TIME: 10 MINUTES | COOKING TIME: 15 MINUTES | SERVES: 2

It's hard to beat mushrooms and bacon in a creamy sauce. This is one of my favourite meals to make – it's quick, easy, and so delicious. This recipe will work with almost any pasta shape, long or short, but this time I've gone for fettuccine.

INGREDIENTS

220g fettuccine

150g bacon lardons

40g butter

300g chestnut mushrooms, cut into quarters

4 cloves of garlic, chopped

120ml vegetable stock

150ml double cream

50g parmesan, grated

15g parsley, chopped

METHOD

1. Cook the pasta in salted boiling water for 2 minutes less than the packet states.

2. Add the bacon lardons into a dry pan and cook over a medium to high heat until crispy.

3. When crispy, use a slotted spoon to remove the lardons from the pan and set aside. Leave the fat in the pan.

4. Add the butter and turn the heat up to high. Chuck in the mushrooms and cook for about 5 minutes, stirring occasionally until they are browned all over.

5. Add in the garlic and cook for a further minute.

6. Turn the heat back down to medium to high, then pour in the vegetable stock and double cream. Add the crisped-up lardons.

7. Bring to the boil. By now, the pasta should be al dente. Add the pasta to the sauce along with some pasta water.

8. Grate in the parmesan and stir well. Season to taste – it will need a bit of black pepper.

9. Turn off the heat and sprinkle in the chopped parsley. Toss together, then plate up and serve with more grated parmesan.

MUSSEL LINGUINE

PREP TIME: 10 MINUTES | COOKING TIME: 15 MINUTES | SERVES: 2

Picture this: it's the height of summer, you fancy a classic seafood pasta, and you fancy it fast. This is it. If you love mussels, you'll be pleased to know that this restaurant-quality pasta dish is quick and easy to make. Mussels are also cheap to buy, so this dish is super low cost. What a bonus.

INGREDIENTS

1kg mussels

200g linguine

4 cloves of garlic, chopped

1 red chilli, thinly sliced

1 tsp dried thyme

½ bunch of parsley, finely chopped, stalks and leaves separated

150ml white wine

250ml tomato passata

METHOD

1. Clean the mussels under cold running water, scrubbing the shells well and removing the hairy beards. Discard any mussels that are already open.

2. Cook the pasta in salted boiling water for 2 minutes less than the packet states.

3. Heat a teaspoon of oil in a large frying pan over a medium heat. Add the garlic, chilli, thyme, and parsley stalks. Cook for a minute.

4. Add the mussels, then pour in the white wine. Cover the pan with a lid or tin foil and cook until the mussels have opened. Discard any that don't open.

5. Remove the mussels from the pan and take half of them out from the shells. Discard the empty shells.

6. Add the deshelled mussels back into the pan, then pour in the passata. Warm the sauce through and add the drained pasta along with a little pasta water.

7. Stir through the chopped parsley leaves and season to taste.

8. Add the remaining mussels on top and serve immediately.

ORZO WITH PEAS & PANCETTA

PREP TIME: 10 MINUTES | COOKING TIME: 15 MINUTES | SERVES: 4

Orzo is a type of short-cut pasta that takes its name from the Italian word for barley. It may resemble rice, but don't be fooled: orzo cooks similarly to many of your favourite pastas. It's super versatile and can be cooked as a midweek dinner or for when you have guests to impress.

INGREDIENTS

150g pancetta

2 cloves of garlic, chopped

300g orzo pasta

600ml chicken stock

150g frozen peas

25g butter

40g parmesan, grated, plus extra for serving

10g parsley, chopped

METHOD

1. Add the pancetta into a large frying pan and turn to a high heat. You don't need to add any oil as the pancetta will release fat.

2. When the pancetta is crispy, add the garlic and cook for a further minute.

3. Add the orzo pasta and give it a stir. Pour in the chicken stock and bring it to a boil. Then, turn down to a simmer for about 8 to 9 minutes, stirring occasionally to make sure it's not sticking.

4. When it's ready, the pasta should be soft, and the liquid absorbed. Now, add the frozen peas, butter, and parmesan. Stir well and cook until the butter has melted.

5. Season to taste, then stir through the chopped parsley. Serve with extra grated parmesan over the top.

PENNE WITH CHICKEN & CHORIZO

PREP TIME: 10 MINUTES | COOKING TIME: 15 MINUTES | SERVES: 2

Creamy chicken and chorizo pasta is the kind of treat that can make any day better. Loaded with crispy bits of chorizo and tender chicken, and smothered in a velvety, super flavourful tomato and cream sauce, this easy chorizo pasta takes less than 30 minutes to make.

INGREDIENTS

200g penne

120g chorizo, chopped into small pieces

1 chicken breast, diced

½ red onion, diced

½ red pepper, diced

3 cloves of garlic, chopped

200ml chicken stock

1 tbsp tomato paste

200g mascarpone

1 bunch of basil, chopped

Parmesan, grated

METHOD

1. Cook the pasta in salted boiling water for 2 minutes less than the packet states.
2. Heat some oil in a large frying pan over a medium to high heat. Cook the chorizo, stirring occasionally, until it starts to turn crispy.
3. Add the diced chicken and cook for a few minutes until it's almost cooked through.
4. Next, add the diced red onion and pepper. Cook for a minute, then chuck in the chopped garlic. Cook for another minute.
5. Pour in the chicken stock and add the tomato paste.
6. Stir through the mascarpone and season to taste.
7. Drain the pasta once cooked but save some of the pasta water.
8. Add the pasta to the sauce and stir to coat. Add a little pasta water to the sauce if it needs loosening up. Toss through the basil.
9. Dish it up and finish with grated parmesan.

PORK & FENNEL RAGÙ

PREP TIME: 10 MINUTES | COOKING TIME: 30 MINUTES | SERVES: 4

This tasty pork ragù with rich passata and fragrant fennel is a flavour bomb that can be ready in 30 minutes.

INGREDIENTS

500g minced pork

2 tsp fennel seeds

100ml red wine

1 onion, diced

1 large carrot, diced

2 celery stalks, diced

4 cloves of garlic, finely chopped

100ml milk

500ml tomato passata

1 tbsp tomato paste

400g pasta

15g parsley, chopped

Parmesan, to serve

METHOD

1. Heat some oil in a large frying pan over a high heat. Add the minced pork, then use a wooden spoon or a whisk to break up the meat as small as you can.

2. Cook over a high heat, stirring often until the meat has browned all over. Turn down to a medium to high heat and keep cooking and stirring until the fat starts to disappear. The pork should start to caramelise and turn golden.

3. Once golden, add the fennel seeds and cook for a further minute before pouring in the red wine to deglaze the pan. Reduce by half, then turn off the heat.

4. Next, heat some oil in a heavy-bottomed pan over a medium to high heat. Add the diced onion, carrot, and celery and cook for 5 minutes until it starts to soften.

5. Add the garlic and cook for a minute more, then add the minced pork and stir well.

6. Pour in the milk, passata, and tomato paste and bring to the boil. Turn down to a simmer for about 15 minutes until the ragù thickens. Season to taste.

7. Meanwhile, cook the pasta in salted boiling water for 2 minutes less than the packet states.

8. Drain the pasta, but reserve some of the pasta water. Add the pasta to the ragù and stir well to coat. Add some pasta water if it needs loosening up.

9. Stir through the chopped parsley, then dish it up and serve with grated parmesan.

PRAWN LINGUINE

PREP TIME: 10 MINUTES | COOKING TIME: 15 MINUTES | SERVES: 2

This is my version of a dish we used to make in the first restaurant I ever worked in. It was the most popular pasta dish on the menu, featuring prawns cooked in a sweet tomato sauce and finished with peppery rocket. The linguine works perfectly with this dish (and if you haven't tried linguine before, it's like a bigger, flatter spaghetti).

INGREDIENTS

200g linguine

80g fennel, thinly sliced

1 red chilli, finely chopped

4 cloves of garlic, finely chopped

80g brown crab meat

400ml tomato passata

300g cherry tomatoes, cut into halves and quarters

300g raw king prawns, peeled

100g rocket

METHOD

1. Cook the pasta in salted boiling water for 2 minutes less than the packet states.

2. In a large frying pan, add a splash of oil and turn to a medium to high heat. When the oil is hot, add the thinly sliced fennel and cook for a minute until softened.

3. Add the chilli and garlic and continue to cook for another minute.

4. Add the brown crab meat and mix well.

5. Pour in the passata and throw in half of the cherry tomatoes.

6. Turn down to a simmer for 3 to 4 minutes.

7. Drain the pasta but keep a little bit of the pasta water back. Add the pasta, pasta water, and prawns into the pan and toss to coat. The prawns will turn pink once cooked through.

8. Throw in the remaining cherry tomatoes and half of the rocket and stir well.

9. Serve the pasta in a bowl, then dress the remaining rocket with olive oil and place it on top to garnish. Serve immediately.

SPAGHETTI BOLOGNESE WITH CRUNCHY PANGRATTATO

PREP TIME: 15 MINUTES | COOKING TIME: 1 HOUR 45 MINUTES | SERVES: 4

Italians adhere to strict rules when preparing their dishes, so changes are not taken favourably. This recipe is a twist on the original so, for argument's sake, let's say this bolognese is inspired by its traditional counterpart. The inclusion of pangrattato, also known as poor man's parmesan, makes this dish extra special. Once you've tried it, you'll be making it time and time again.

INGREDIENTS

FOR THE BOLOGNESE

400g minced beef

200g minced pork

1 large onion, diced

2 carrots, diced

2 celery stalks, diced

1 bunch of rosemary, chopped

3 bay leaves

4 tsp chopped garlic

180ml red wine

200ml beef stock

2 tbsp tomato paste

2 x 400g tins of chopped tomatoes

FOR THE PANGRATTATO

2 tbsp olive oil

1 bunch of rosemary, chopped

1 bunch of thyme, chopped

2 tsp chopped garlic

100g fresh breadcrumbs

TO SERVE

400g spaghetti

Parmesan

METHOD

1. Add the minced beef and minced pork to a large pan. Cook over a high heat, using a wooden spoon or a spatula to break up the meat.

2. Keep cooking the mince until it has browned all over and all the liquid has disappeared.

3. Add the onion, carrot, and celery to the pan. Cook for a few minutes, then add the rosemary, bay leaves and chopped garlic. Mix well and cook for a further minute.

4. Pour in the red wine and reduce by half. Add the beef stock.

5. Stir well, then add the tomato paste and the tins of chopped tomatoes.

6. Turn down to a simmer for about 90 minutes until you have a thick, rich sauce. Season to taste.

7. While it's cooking, you can prepare the pangrattato. In a large frying pan, heat up the olive oil and add the rosemary, thyme and chopped garlic. Fry for 1 minute before adding the breadcrumbs.

8. Cook over a high heat, stirring constantly until the breadcrumbs have turned golden and crunchy. Place them into a bowl and set aside.

9. When the ragù is almost ready, cook your pasta in salted boiling water for 2 minutes less than the packet states.

10. Once the pasta is al dente, toss it with the ragù and add some pasta water to loosen the sauce.

11. Dish it up and grate some parmesan over the top.

12. Finish with the crunchy pangrattato.

SPICY NDUJA PASTA WITH CREAMY BURRATA

PREP TIME: 10 MINUTES | COOKING TIME: 15 MINUTES | SERVES: 2

Nduja and burrata are two incredible ingredients that don't quite get the love that they deserve. Nduja is a spicy, spreadable pork sausage that originates from the Calabria region in the south of Italy. Burrata, also from the south, is an Italian cow's milk cheese made from mozzarella and cream. This pairing is a marriage made in heaven.

INGREDIENTS

200g pasta (I use rigatoni)

1 red onion, diced

2 tbsp vegetable oil

60g nduja

3 cloves of garlic, chopped

100ml red wine

400ml tomato passata

1 bunch of fresh basil

2 x 150g burrata (drained weight)

Parmesan, grated

METHOD

1. Drop the pasta into salted boiling water and cook for 2 minutes less than the packet states.

2. Meanwhile, heat some oil in a large frying pan and cook the onions for a few minutes over a medium to high heat until they start to soften.

3. Add the oil to the nduja and use a fork to mash it up a bit.

4. Add the nduja to the pan and cook for a couple of minutes to release the flavours.

5. Chuck in the garlic and cook for 1 more minute before pouring in the red wine. Cook until the wine has reduced by half.

6. Pour in the passata and use a ladle to add in some of the seasoned pasta water. Stir well and cook over a medium heat for a few minutes.

7. Once the pasta is al dente, drain it and add it to the sauce. Add some of the pasta water if you need to loosen the sauce.

8. Tear in the basil leaves and stir through. Season to taste.

9. Dish it up and pop a ball of burrata atop each portion.

10. Grate over some parmesan cheese and serve immediately.

SPINACH & RICOTTA STUFFED SHELLS

PREP TIME: 10 MINUTES | COOKING TIME: 40 MINUTES | SERVES: 4

In this easy Spinach and Ricotta Stuffed Shells recipe, three cheeses combine with quick sautéed spinach, marinara sauce, and jumbo pasta shells for a hearty, comforting, and crowd-pleasing vegetarian dinner.

INGREDIENTS

16 jumbo pasta shells (plus a couple extra as some may break while the pasta cooks)

1 onion, diced

4 tsp chopped garlic

200g baby spinach, roughly chopped

340g ricotta

80g parmesan, grated, plus more for serving

1 large egg

1 bunch of fresh basil, chopped

½ tsp salt

½ tsp black pepper

600ml tomato passata

200g mozzarella, grated

METHOD

1. Preheat the oven to 190°c.

2. Cook the pasta in salted boiling water for 2 minutes less than the packet states. Drain when ready, then run cold water over the pasta shells. Once cooled, set aside.

3. Meanwhile, heat some oil in a large pan over a medium to high heat. Add the onion and cook for about 4 to 5 minutes until softened.

4. Add the garlic and cook for another minute. Add the spinach and cook, stirring occasionally, until the leaves begin to wilt but are still bright green, about 2 to 3 minutes. The spinach should be reduced by half. Remove from the heat and cool.

5. In a mixing bowl, stir together the spinach, ricotta, grated parmesan, egg, basil, salt and pepper until well combined.

6. Pour half of the tomato passata into the bottom of a suitable baking dish. Stuff each pasta shell with a generous amount of the spinach and ricotta mixture, then place them in the baking dish.

7. Cover with the remaining passata, then sprinkle over the grated mozzarella. Bake it for 25 minutes until the top begins to brown and the sauce is bubbling.

8. Serve warm with lots of grated parmesan.

SUPER GREEN PASTA

PREP TIME: 10 MINUTES | COOKING TIME: 15 MINUTES | SERVES: 2

Who knew that using hummus made such a fabulous, quick, and creamy pasta sauce? Simply blitz all the ingredients together until silky smooth, then stir through farfalle (bowtie) pasta for an easy midweek meal.

INGREDIENTS

200g farfalle

100g hummus

1 avocado, roughly chopped

100ml light coconut milk

100g frozen peas

1 bunch of basil, torn

1 bunch of mint, leaves removed

1 lemon, zested and juiced

140g tinned sweetcorn, drained

Parmesan, grated

METHOD

1. Cook the pasta in salted boiling water for 2 minutes less than the packet states.

2. Put the hummus, avocado, coconut milk, peas, mint, basil, and the zest and juice of the lemon into a blender and blitz until completely smooth and bright green.

3. Drain the pasta once cooked, but reserve some of the pasta water. Add the drained pasta into a pan and pour in the Super Green sauce along with a little pasta water.

4. Add the sweetcorn and toss together over a medium heat to warm through. Don't heat too much, though – think of it as a saucy pesto. Season to taste.

5. Dish it up and serve with a little grated parmesan.

TAGLIATELLE PRIMAVERA

PREP TIME: 10 MINUTES | COOKING TIME: 15 MINUTES | SERVES: 2

Primavera means 'springtime' in Italian, and that's exactly what this pasta dish represents. It uses spring vegetables to create a creamy pasta sauce that'll make you forget all about meat. With the addition of lemon and mascarpone, this dish becomes a springtime flavour explosion.

INGREDIENTS

200g tagliatelle

1 onion, finely diced

4 cloves of garlic, chopped

1 red chilli, finely sliced

100g courgette, diced

120g asparagus, finely sliced

120ml white wine

120g cherry tomatoes, cut into quarters

120g frozen peas

120g frozen broad beans

80g mascarpone

2 lemons

½ bunch of fresh parsley, finely chopped

½ bunch of fresh mint, finely chopped

Parmesan, grated

METHOD

1. Cook the pasta in salted boiling water for 2 minutes less than the packet states.

2. Heat some cooking oil in a large frying pan, add the onion and cook for a few minutes until it starts to soften.

3. Add the garlic, chilli, courgette, and asparagus, and cook for a further 2 minutes.

4. Pour in the white wine and reduce it by half. Once reduced, add the cherry tomatoes, peas and broad beans.

5. Use tongs to add the pasta into the sauce, adding pasta water as you do so. Toss it all together.

6. Add the mascarpone, zest and juice of one lemon, and the chopped mint and parsley. Mix it all together and season to taste.

7. Serve stacked high in a pasta bowl and finish with grated parmesan and more lemon zest.

TUNA PASTA BAKE

PREP TIME: 15 MINUTES | COOKING TIME: 30 MINUTES | SERVES: 4

Everybody should have a wickedly delicious Tuna Pasta Bake recipe up their sleeve. This version is full of flavour and bears no resemblance to the usual acts of desperation associated with tinned tuna meals. You can substitute the mozzarella for cheddar if you like, but I often opt for the mozzarella as it turns a lovely golden brown.

INGREDIENTS

300g fusilli

1 onion, diced

4 cloves of garlic, chopped

2 x 400g tins of chopped tomatoes

1 tbsp tomato paste

1 tbsp oregano

435g tinned tuna (net weight, approx. 3 standard tins)

200g mozzarella, grated

METHOD

1. Preheat the oven to 180°c.

2. Cook the pasta in salted boiling water for 2 minutes less than the packet states. Once cooked, drain in a colander and run under cold water to stop it sticking together.

3. To make the sauce, heat a little oil over a medium to high heat. Add the onion and cook for a few minutes until it starts to soften.

4. Add the garlic and cook for a further minute, then pour in the tinned tomatoes, tomato paste, 180ml of water, and oregano.

5. Bring to the boil and then turn down to a simmer. Cook for 5 minutes, stirring occasionally.

6. Season with salt and black pepper, then take it off the heat and add the cooked pasta, stirring to combine.

7. Add the drained tuna and gently stir it through, being careful not to break it up too much.

8. Tip the pasta into a suitably sized baking dish and top with the grated mozzarella.

9. Bake for 20 minutes or until golden on top.

10. Leave to stand for a few minutes before serving.

VEGGIE WONDERS

Vegetarianism as a dietary lifestyle has been growing in popularity in recent years, with many people choosing to eliminate or reduce their consumption of meat and animal products for health, ethical, or environmental reasons.

Vegetarian cooking offers a wide range of flavours, textures and ingredients to choose from, making it an exciting and delicious way to eat. In this section of the cookbook, you'll find lots of simple recipes that cater to a vegetarian diet.

GREEN BEAN, POTATO & HALLOUMI TRAYBAKE

PREP TIME: 10 MINUTES | COOKING TIME: 40 MINUTES | SERVES: 4

Simplicity is the name of the game with this veggie traybake. Halloumi is always a top choice, and this traybake has enough greens to keep it healthy, but enough potato chunks to make it hearty. This meal proves that even simple food can be mouth-wateringly delicious.

INGREDIENTS

700g baby potatoes, halved and quartered

6 cloves of garlic, skin-on and bashed

4 tbsp olive oil

200g green beans, halved

225g halloumi, cut into 2cm cubes

1 lemon, zested and juiced

30g basil, torn

METHOD

1. Preheat the oven to 180°c.
2. Put the potatoes and garlic into a large roasting tray. Add the olive oil, season with salt and pepper and toss well. Roast for 30 minutes.
3. Remove the roasting tray from the oven, add the green beans and halloumi and toss to combine. You don't want the tray to be too crowded – everything should be in a single layer.
4. Return the tray to the oven for 15 minutes, or until the beans are tender and the halloumi has started to caramelise.
5. Discard the garlic, then add the zest and the juice of the lemon and toss together.
6. Transfer to a serving dish and scatter over the torn basil leaves.

MINESTRONE SOUP

PREP TIME: 15 MINUTES | COOKING TIME: 25 MINUTES | SERVES: 4

This Italian vegetable soup, with its rich tomato base, pasta, and beans, is both classic and comforting. Not only that, but it's low in calories and packed with fibre and vitamin C.

INGREDIENTS

1 onion, diced

2 medium sized carrots, diced

3 celery stalks, diced

2 tsp oregano

2 bay leaves

4 cloves of garlic, finely chopped

2 tbsp tomato paste

1 x 400g tin of chopped tomatoes

1 litre vegetable stock

200g potato, diced

1 x 400g tin of haricot beans

100g small pasta (I used chifferi rigati)

¼ head of Savoy cabbage, shredded

1 red pepper, diced

1 bunch of fresh basil, torn

TO SERVE

Parmesan, grated

Bread

METHOD

1. Place a large saucepan over a medium heat, add a little oil, then add the onion, carrot, celery, oregano, and bay leaves. Cook for about 10 minutes, stirring occasionally, until the vegetables have softened.

2. Add the chopped garlic and cook for a further minute. Stir in the tomato paste then cook for another minute.

3. Pour in the chopped tinned tomatoes and the vegetable stock. Add the diced potato.

4. Bring to the boil, then turn down to a simmer and cook for 10 minutes.

5. Add the haricot beans and the pasta. Cook for a further 10 minutes, or until the pasta has cooked.

6. If it starts to look dry, just add a bit of water. Once the pasta has cooked, stir in the cabbage and red pepper. Season to taste then cook for 2 more minutes.

7. Stir in the fresh basil and serve with grated parmesan and some chunks of bread.

GNOCCHI & TOMATO BAKE

PREP TIME: 5 MINUTES | COOKING TIME: 20 MINUTES | SERVES: 4

If you've never heard of gnocchi, they're essentially little Italian dumplings. The dough is made using flour, eggs, and potato, but you can find ready-made gnocchi in any big supermarket. Try this simple gnocchi traybake, topped with cheddar and mozzarella, and get ready to fight over those moreish crispy edges!

INGREDIENTS

1 x 400g tin of chopped tomatoes

2 tbsp tomato paste

4 cloves of garlic, chopped

250g cherry tomatoes, halved

30g basil, roughly chopped

600g gnocchi

100ml vegetable stock

150g cheddar, grated

250g mozzarella, torn into chunks

METHOD

1. Preheat the oven to 200°c.

2. In a large mixing bowl, add the chopped tomatoes, tomato paste, garlic, cherry tomatoes, basil, and half of the gnocchi. Season with salt and black pepper, pour in the vegetable stock and stir well.

3. Tip it into a large ovenproof baking dish, then add the remaining gnocchi on top. Sprinkle over the grated cheddar and torn mozzarella.

4. Bake in the oven for 20 minutes or until it's golden and crisp.

CREAMY MUSHROOM SOUP

PREP TIME: 10 MINUTES | COOKING TIME: 30 MINUTES | SERVES: 4

This homemade Creamy Mushroom Soup is full of flavour and so easy to make – you won't buy tinned soup again! The Marsala wine adds a real depth of flavour, making this one extra special. Serve with garlic ciabatta toast, topped with pan fried mushrooms.

INGREDIENTS

40g butter

2 onions, diced

4 cloves of garlic, chopped

750g chestnut mushrooms, sliced

30g fresh thyme, chopped

120ml Marsala wine (or any dry red or white wine)

40g plain flour

600ml vegetable stock

240ml double cream

20g parsley, chopped

FOR THE TOASTED CIABATTA

1 ciabatta

3 cloves of garlic (1 whole, 2 chopped)

150g shiitake mushrooms

5g parsley, chopped

METHOD

1. Add the butter and some oil to a large heavy-bottomed pan over a medium to high heat.

2. Once melted, add the onions, and cook until they start to soften.

3. Chuck in the garlic and cook for a further minute, then add the mushrooms and thyme. Cook for 5 more minutes, stirring occasionally.

4. Once the mushrooms have softened, pour in the wine and reduce by half.

5. Stir in the plain flour, mix well, and cook for 2 minutes before pouring in the vegetable stock.

6. Bring to the boil, then turn down to a simmer. Cover and cook for 5 minutes.

7. Pour in the cream and allow to gently simmer for a further 5 to 10 minutes.

8. Season to taste. It will need a good amount of salt and black pepper.

9. Stir through the chopped parsley.

FOR THE TOASTED GARLIC CIABATTA

1. Slice the ciabatta into 1cm thick slices. Pop in the toaster until golden and crisp, then rub the whole garlic clove over each slice so it melts into the toast.

2. Heat oil and butter in a large frying pan over a high heat. Add the mushrooms and cook for 4 to 5 minutes, stirring occasionally until they soften.

3. Add the garlic and chopped parsley and cook for a further minute.

4. Lay the garlicky mushrooms over the toasted ciabatta and serve alongside the soup.

DID YOU KNOW...?

CARROTS WERE ORIGINALLY PURPLE

As a tribute to William of Orange, Dutch
growers in the late 16th century took mutant
strains of the purple carrot and gradually
developed them into the sweet, plump, orange
variety that are popular today. Before this,
pretty much all carrots were purple.

VEGETABLE PILAU

PREP TIME: 10 MINUTES | COOKING TIME: 25 MINUTES | SERVES: 4

Pilau rice originates from South Asia and the Middle East. Traditionally, long grain rice is cooked in stock and spices to create a fragrant, fluffy rice. This recipe adds warming spices and lots of vegetables to create a deliciously easy one-pot meal.

INGREDIENTS

240g basmati rice

20g butter

1 cinnamon stick

5 whole cloves

4 cardamom pods, lightly crushed

1 star anise

1 onion, finely sliced

1 tsp ground turmeric

1 tsp ground cumin

½ tsp red chilli powder

450ml water

75g green beans

150g cauliflower, cut into florets

1 large carrot, finely diced

100g frozen peas

30g pistachios

METHOD

1. Place the rice into a sieve and run under cold water. Run your fingers through to wash the grains, drain well, then set aside. This step washes off some of the starch and stops the grains of rice sticking together.

2. Heat the butter and some oil in a large heavy-bottomed pan over a medium to high heat. Once the butter has melted, add the cinnamon, cloves, cardamom, and star anise. Fry for a minute until they crackle and start to smell fragrant.

3. Add the onions and fry for 4 to 5 minutes, stirring occasionally until they start to soften.

4. Stir in the turmeric, cumin, and chilli powder, and cook for a further minute.

5. Add the rice into the pan, then pour in the water and season with a large pinch of salt.

6. Chuck in the green beans, cauliflower, carrot, and peas and stir well. Turn down to a simmer then cover with a lid and cook for about 10 to 12 minutes, or until the rice is cooked and the water has been absorbed.

7. Turn off the heat and leave to steam for a further 5 minutes.

8. Uncover and use a fork to fluff up the rice. Finish with the chopped pistachios and serve.

MIXED BEAN CHILLI

PREP TIME: 10 MINUTES | COOKING TIME: 30 MINUTES | SERVES: 4

Here's my recipe for a one-pot mixed bean chilli that's super easy to make, healthy and delicious. It uses aromatic Mexican spices to give it a smoky, rich flavour, and is packed with vitamins, complex carbohydrates, protein, and fibre.

INGREDIENTS

1 red onion, diced

1 red pepper, diced

4 cloves of garlic, chopped

1 tbsp ground cumin

1 tbsp smoked paprika

1 tbsp chipotle paste

1 x 400g tin of chopped tomatoes

500ml vegetable stock

1 tbsp oregano

1 tbsp soft brown sugar

3 x 400g tins of mixed beans

20g coriander, chopped

TO GARNISH

Lime wedges

Soured cream

METHOD

1. Add a little bit of oil to a large saucepan and turn to a medium to high heat. Cook the onion and red pepper for about 4 to 5 minutes, stirring occasionally until softened.

2. Chuck in the garlic and cook for a further minute, then add the cumin and paprika. Cook for another 30 seconds.

3. Stir in the chipotle paste, tin of tomatoes, vegetable stock, oregano, and soft brown sugar.

4. Bring to the boil, add the beans, then turn down to a simmer and cook for about 20 minutes. You may need to add a little water as you go if the chilli becomes too thick.

5. Sprinkle over the chopped coriander and season to taste. Dish it up with rice or sweet potato wedges, garnish with soured cream, and serve with a wedge of lime.

SWEET POTATO KATSU CURRY

PREP TIME: 20 MINUTES | COOKING TIME: 25 MINUTES | SERVES: 2

Katsu curry is one of Japan's best-loved dishes. It typically consists of crunchy, breadcrumb-coated vegetables or meat cloaked in a gently spiced, sweet sauce. Here, I've used sweet potato for a delicious Veggie Wonder version. Serve with a fresh, crunchy side salad and sticky rice.

INGREDIENTS

FOR THE SWEET POTATO

1 large sweet potato

100g plain flour

2 eggs, lightly beaten

100g panko breadcrumbs

FOR THE CURRY SAUCE

1 onion, diced

1 carrot, sliced

4 cloves of garlic, chopped

1 thumb-sized piece of ginger, minced

2 tsp turmeric

2 tsp curry powder

1 x 400ml tin of coconut milk

200ml vegetable stock

1 tbsp soy sauce

2 tbsp honey

FOR THE SALAD

1 carrot

1 cucumber

50g radish

80g spring onions

20ml rice wine vinegar

METHOD

FOR THE SWEET POTATO

1. Preheat the oven to 180°c.

2. Peel the sweet potato and slice into 0.5cm rounds.

3. Coat each round in the flour, then the egg, and finally in the panko breadcrumbs.

4. Place the coated sweet potato onto a lined baking tray and bake for 20 minutes.

FOR THE CURRY SAUCE

1. Add the onion, carrot, garlic, and ginger to a pan over a medium heat. Cook until the onions and carrot start to soften.

2. Add the turmeric and curry powder, stir, and cook for 2 minutes.

3. Pour in the coconut milk and vegetable stock.

4. Turn the heat to low and simmer until it has reduced by half and the carrots have softened. Add a little water if the sauce needs loosening up.

5. Use a stick blender to blitz the sauce to a smooth consistency.

6. Add the soy sauce and honey, stir well, then season to taste.

FOR THE SALAD

1. Thinly slice the carrot, cucumber, radish, and spring onion and add to a bowl.

2. Toss the salad with the rice wine vinegar.

TO SERVE

1. Dish up the crunchy katsu sweet potato with sticky rice, then spoon over some of the curry sauce. Serve the salad on the side.

MUSHROOM RISOTTO

PREP TIME: 25 MINUTES | COOKING TIME: 30 MINUTES | SERVES: 2

This decadent porcini and wild mushroom risotto is topped with buffalo mozzarella and grated parmesan. The dried porcini mushrooms create a greater depth of flavour that makes this a wonderful dish for impressing your dinner guests, or even having as a weeknight treat.

INGREDIENTS

25g dried porcini mushrooms

400ml vegetable stock

1 onion, diced

1 bunch of thyme, chopped

150g risotto rice

80ml white wine

50g butter

50g parmesan, grated

1 bunch of parsley, chopped

200g wild mushrooms (such as oyster and shiitake)

4 cloves of garlic, chopped

50g buffalo mozzarella

METHOD

1. Place the dried porcini mushrooms into a jug or bowl and pour over 400ml of boiling water. Leave them to soak for 20 minutes.

2. Pour the vegetable stock into a saucepan, then use a sieve to drain the porcini stock into the vegetable stock. Place the stock over a medium heat.

3. Squeeze the porcini dry, then roughly chop and set aside.

4. Pour some oil into a large frying pan and turn to a medium to high heat. Add the diced onion and chopped thyme and cook for about 5 minutes until the onions have softened.

5. Turn up the heat and add the risotto rice. Toast the rice for a few minutes, stirring occasionally, until it starts to crackle and pop.

6. Pour in the wine (it should sizzle) and reduce by half.

7. Add the chopped porcini to the pan, then add the stock a ladle at a time, stirring continuously. Once the previous ladleful of stock has been absorbed, add another.

8. Repeat this for about 15 to 20 minutes until the rice has cooked but still has a slight bite. Don't worry if you haven't used all the stock.

9. Turn off the heat and stir in the butter, parmesan, and half of the chopped parsley. Season to taste.

10. In another frying pan, heat some oil and a little bit of butter over a high heat. Add the wild mushrooms and cook for a few minutes until they start to soften.

11. Add the chopped garlic and cook for a further minute. Turn off the heat, season to taste, then add the rest of the chopped parsley.

12. Serve the risotto in a bowl and top with the pan fried mushrooms.

13. Tear the mozzarella and spread it over the risotto, then finish with some parmesan shavings.

SHAKSHUKA

PREP TIME: 10 MINUTES | COOKING TIME: 25 MINUTES | SERVES: 4

Shakshuka is an easy, healthy breakfast recipe (or brunch, lunch, or dinner) that is popular in Israel and other parts of the Middle East and North Africa. It's a simple combination of tomatoes, onions, garlic, spices, and gently poached eggs. It's nourishing, filling, and a recipe that I guarantee you'll make time and time again.

INGREDIENTS

1 onion, diced

1 red pepper, diced

4 cloves of garlic, chopped

1 red chilli, chopped

1 tsp cumin

2 tsp smoked paprika

2 x 400g tins of chopped tomatoes

1 tbsp tomato paste

1 tbsp soft brown sugar

6 eggs

Fresh parsley, to serve

METHOD

1. Start by frying the diced onion over a medium to high heat for 2 to 3 minutes until it starts to soften.

2. Add the diced pepper and cook for 1 more minute, stirring occasionally.

3. Add the chopped garlic and chilli, followed by the cumin and smoked paprika.

4. Cook for 1 minute before pouring in the chopped tomatoes and adding the tomato paste.

5. Season with salt and pepper and add the soft brown sugar.

6. Simmer over a medium heat for 10 to 15 minutes until the sauce has thickened.

7. Make six small pockets in the sauce and crack an egg into each.

8. Cover the pan with a lid or tin foil and simmer for 6 to 8 minutes, or until the eggs have cooked.

9. Scatter the fresh parsley over the top and serve with toasted sourdough.

PANEER, CHICKPEA & SPINACH CURRY

PREP TIME: 10 MINUTES | COOKING TIME: 10 MINUTES | SERVES: 4

Don't wait for the weekend to enjoy a curry. This quick recipe combines paneer cheese, chickpeas, and spinach for a tasty, warming dinner. If you haven't tried it before, paneer is a mild, non-melting cheese that's popular in Indian cooking. It has a similar squeaky texture to halloumi.

INGREDIENTS

225g paneer

1 onion, diced

1 tbsp curry powder

1 tsp garlic paste

1 tsp ginger paste

1 x 400g tin of chopped tomatoes

200ml milk

1 x 400g tin of chickpeas

200g baby spinach

TO SERVE

Basmati rice

Naan breads

METHOD

1. Cut the paneer into 1.5cm cubes.

2. Heat some oil in a large pan, then cook the diced onion over a medium to high heat for about 5 to 6 minutes until it starts to soften.

3. Add the curry powder, garlic paste and ginger paste, then cook for a minute to release the flavours.

4. Pour in the tin of chopped tomatoes and the milk. Stir well and bring to a simmer.

5. Add the diced paneer, chickpeas, and baby spinach. The spinach may look like a lot, but it will quickly wilt and reduce.

6. Simmer for 5 minutes, then season to taste. It will need a little salt and black pepper.

7. Dish it up with basmati rice and naan breads.

CHAMPION SIDES

Side dishes are an integral part of any meal and often play a crucial role in rounding out the flavours and textures of a dish. They can be simple or complex, hearty or light, and can be made with a variety of ingredients, including vegetables, grains, and legumes. Whether you're looking to add some colour to your plate, or just want to make a meal more filling, there's a side dish to suit every taste and occasion.

CAJUN RICE

PREP TIME: 10 MINUTES | COOKING TIME: 30 MINUTES | SERVES: 4

Cajun cuisine is known for its bold and spicy flavours, and this rice recipe is no exception. This dish combines long grain rice with a mixture of Cajun spices, onions, and peppers to create a savoury and satisfying main course or side dish.

INGREDIENTS

1 onion, diced

1 red pepper, diced

1 carrot, diced

2 celery stalks, diced

4 cloves of garlic, chopped

2 tbsp Cajun seasoning

240g long grain rice

500ml vegetable stock

50g spring onions, sliced

10g parsley, chopped

METHOD

1. Heat some oil in a large heavy-bottomed pan. Add the diced onion, pepper, carrot, and celery and cook over a medium to high heat for about 5 minutes, stirring occasionally.

2. Chuck in the garlic and Cajun seasoning and cook for a further minute.

3. Add the rice and stir well. Pour in the vegetable stock and season with salt. Cover with a lid and leave to simmer for 20 minutes, or until the rice is cooked and the water has evaporated.

4. Turn off the heat and leave to stand for 5 minutes, then use a fork to fluff up the rice.

5. Scatter over the spring onions and chopped parsley and serve.

CAPRESE ROASTED ASPARAGUS

PREP TIME: 5 MINUTES | COOKING TIME: 10 MINUTES | SERVES: 2

Make asparagus even more exciting by combining it with the delicious flavours of a classic Italian caprese salad. This one's perfect as a dinner party starter or a side dish.

INGREDIENTS

300g asparagus, trimmed

150g cherry tomatoes, halved

50g mozzarella, grated

TO SERVE

Balsamic glaze

15g fresh basil, torn

METHOD

1. Preheat the oven to 200°c.

2. Add the asparagus and tomatoes to an oven tray, drizzle over a little olive oil, and sprinkle over a pinch of salt.

3. Roast for 5 minutes.

4. Remove from the oven and sprinkle over the grated mozzarella. Place back into the oven and roast for 5 more minutes, or until the cheese has melted and is slightly golden.

5. Serve the roasted asparagus with a drizzle of balsamic glaze and the torn basil.

COURGETTE FRITTERS

PREP TIME: 5 MINUTES | COOKING TIME: 10 MINUTES | SERVES: 4

These cheesy courgette fritters have a crispy outside and a fluffy, cheesy centre. They're a perfect way to make eating veggies less boring.

INGREDIENTS

2 medium courgettes

60g cheddar, grated

½ red onion, finely grated

½ red pepper, diced

1 egg, lightly beaten

80g plain flour

Soured cream

Chopped chives

METHOD

1. Grate the courgettes using a box grater, then squeeze any excess water out of the courgettes with your hands. Add the grated courgette to the bowl along with the rest of the ingredients and stir until combined.

2. Heat some oil in a large frying pan over a medium to high heat. Spoon the mixture into the pan and flatten each portion with the back of the spoon.

3. Cook for 2 to 3 minutes on each side until they are golden.

4. Remove from the pan and set onto kitchen paper to get rid of any excess oil.

5. Serve with a dollop of soured cream and sprinkle with the chopped chives.

MINTY MACHO PEAS

PREP TIME: 5 MINUTES | COOKING TIME: 10 MINUTES | SERVES: 4

This recipe elevates the humble pea by combining it with fresh mint, butter, garlic, and chilli to create a fresh and zesty dish. The mint adds a brightness that complements the sweetness of the peas, while the garlic and butter provide depth and luxuriousness.

INGREDIENTS

50g butter

1 red onion, finely diced

4 cloves of garlic, chopped

1 red chilli, chopped

500g frozen peas

35g fresh mint, chopped

100g spring onions, sliced

1 lemon, zested and juiced

METHOD

1. Melt the butter in a large pan, add the diced red onion and cook over a medium heat for 2 minutes.

2. Add in the garlic and chilli and cook for 30 seconds.

3. Add in the peas and stir well. Pour in 100ml of water and cover with a lid. Bring to the boil. Cook for 2 to 3 minutes.

4. Drain any remaining liquid then stir through the chopped mint, spring onions, and some olive oil. Add the zest and juice of the lemon, stir well, then season with salt and pepper.

TEAR & SHARE GARLIC KNOTS

PREP TIME: 15 MINUTES, PLUS 1 HOUR 30 MINUTES PROVING | COOKING TIME: 40 MINUTES | SERVES: 12

This tasty recipe makes a perfect starter or side dish that's great for sharing with friends and family. It will always provide the wow factor and is guaranteed to impress even the harshest of critics.

INGREDIENTS

500g strong white bread flour

7g sachet of dried yeast

500ml tepid water

340g butter, softened

10 cloves of garlic, crushed

1 bunch of parsley, chopped

100g breadcrumbs

METHOD

1. Combine the flour, yeast, and 1 teaspoon of sea salt in a large mixing bowl.

2. Make a well in the middle of the flour and gradually pour in the water, continuously mixing, and bringing in the flour from the sides.

3. Once combined, tip the dough out onto a floured surface and knead for 10 minutes. The dough should be smooth and springy, not sticky.

4. Cut the dough into approximately 80g portions. Roll into balls and place on a tray a few centimetres apart. Cover the tray in cling film or a damp tea towel and leave to prove for 45 minutes, or until it's doubled in size.

5. Meanwhile, mix the softened butter with the crushed garlic and chopped parsley.

6. Spread a quarter of the garlic butter around a large baking tray (or springform tin) and sprinkle the breadcrumbs over the top.

7. Once the dough has doubled in size, flatten each portion so they're long and thin, then spread garlic butter over the top of each (using another quarter in total). Roll the portions up like mini Swiss rolls and arrange them upright in the greased tray.

8. Cover with cling film or a damp tea towel and leave to prove for another 30 to 45 minutes.

9. Brush with even more garlic butter, then sprinkle some sea salt over the top. Bake in the oven at 190°c for 35 minutes.

10. Remove from the tray and serve. You can melt any remaining garlic butter over the top or serve it as a dip.

TENDERSTEM BROCCOLI WITH CHORIZO

PREP TIME: 5 MINUTES | COOKING TIME: 15 MINUTES | SERVES: 2

Enjoy this flavourful side dish of tenderstem broccoli and chorizo. The crispy chorizo and tender broccoli are perfectly complemented by the garlic and lemon, making this a simple and delicious addition to any meal.

INGREDIENTS

150g chorizo, diced

½ red onion, diced

4 cloves of garlic, minced

200g tenderstem broccoli, trimmed

1 lemon, zested

METHOD

1. Add some oil into a large frying pan and place over a medium to high heat. Add the chorizo and cook for a few minutes until it starts to turn crispy.

2. Add the diced red onion and cook for 2 minutes. Then chuck in the garlic and cook for 1 more minute.

3. Add the trimmed broccoli to the pan and pour in 50ml of water. Cook for about 4 to 5 minutes until the broccoli is tender.

4. Season with salt and pepper, add the zest of the lemon, then squeeze in the juice of half of the lemon and serve immediately.

DID YOU KNOW...?

FIGS CONTAIN DEAD WASPS

As part of the pollination process,
female fig wasps crawl inside of a fig to lay their
eggs and unfortunately die during the process.

But don't worry, by the time we eat
the sweet fruits, there are no traces of
the wasp left as they're fully digested
by the fig.

TWISTY POTATO GRATIN

PREP TIME: 10 MINUTES | COOKING TIME: 1 HOUR 10 MINUTES | SERVES: 6

The twisty cousin of the classic French dish, potato dauphinoise, this gratin is made with tender sliced potatoes that are cooked in a creamy, cheesy sauce. This comforting side dish is perfect for special occasions or whenever you're in the mood for something rich and warming.

INGREDIENTS

200ml whole milk

200ml double cream

1 tsp ground nutmeg

1 tsp garlic granules

1 bunch of thyme, chopped

60g parmesan, grated

1.5kg Maris Piper potatoes

METHOD

1. Preheat the oven to 165°c.

2. Pour the milk and the double cream into a saucepan. Add the nutmeg, garlic granules, chopped thyme, and 40g of the grated parmesan.

3. Cook over a medium heat until it's almost boiling, then take off the heat. Season to taste.

4. Meanwhile, use a mandoline to thinly slice the potatoes.

5. Layer the potatoes, standing them up like dominoes all around an ovenproof dish. (I use a 22cm round pie dish.)

6. Pour the cream mixture over the top, then sprinkle with the remaining parmesan.

7. Bake in the oven for 55 minutes.

8. Turn the heat up to 200°c and cook for a further 10 to 15 minutes or until the potatoes become crispy on top.

9. Leave to stand for 5 minutes before serving.

SALT & PEPPER CHIPS

PREP TIME: 10 MINUTES | COOKING TIME: 45 MINUTES | SERVES: 4

Salt and pepper chips are a classic and delicious snack or side. Using just a few basic ingredients, you too can make these crispy, seasoned chips that are perfect for munching on. This recipe is super easy to follow, so you'll be ready to enjoy these in no time at all!

INGREDIENTS

FOR THE CHIPS

800g Maris Piper potatoes

50g cornflour

1 tsp salt

1 tsp black pepper

1 tsp paprika

2 tbsp vegetable oil

FOR THE SEASONING

1 onion, roughly chopped

1 red chilli, sliced

1 green chilli, sliced

1 tsp salt

1 tsp black pepper

1 tbsp Chinese five spice

5 spring onions, chopped

4 cloves of garlic, minced

METHOD

1. Preheat the oven to 200°c and line a large baking tray with baking paper.

2. Cut the potatoes into chips, leaving the skin on if preferred.

3. Sprinkle the cornflour, salt, pepper and paprika over the chips and toss to coat.

4. Scatter them onto the lined baking tray, spreading them out as much as possible and drizzling them with the oil.

5. Cover them with foil and bake for 10 minutes, then remove the foil and pop them back in for another 20 minutes.

6. Take them out, turn them over, and bake for about 10 more minutes until they are golden and crispy.

7. For the seasoning, heat some oil in a large frying pan or wok over a high heat and stir fry the onion and chilli for 1 minute.

8. Add the salt, pepper and Chinese five spice and cook for another minute.

9. Turn the heat down slightly and add in the spring onions and chopped garlic.

10. Cook for 1 more minute before chucking the chips in and tossing it all together. Dish up and enjoy.

MANGO SLAW

PREP TIME: 10 MINUTES | SERVES: 4

Mango slaw is a colourful and delicious twist on a traditional coleslaw, and it's perfect for summertime. The juicy sweetness of the mango pairs perfectly with the crunchy vegetables and tangy dressing, creating a light, balanced and flavourful dish.

INGREDIENTS

200g red cabbage, finely shredded

2 carrots, grated

100g sugar snap peas, thinly sliced lengthways

2 ripe mangoes, peeled and thinly sliced

2 tbsp extra virgin olive oil

6 tbsp mango chutney

METHOD

1.   Add all the ingredients to a large salad bowl, mix well, and serve.

FONDANT POTATOES

PREP TIME: 10 MINUTES | COOKING TIME: 50 MINUTES | SERVES: 4

This is my favourite way to cook potatoes. Treat yourself with these incredible buttery fondant potatoes infused with garlic and herbs.

INGREDIENTS

1kg Maris Piper potatoes

8 cloves of garlic

150g butter, cubed

4 sprigs of rosemary

4 sprigs of thyme

250ml chicken stock

METHOD

1. Preheat the oven to 180°c.

2. Peel the potatoes and cut them into 1.5-inch rounds. Then, use a cookie cutter to cut out perfect circles.

3. Peel the garlic cloves and crush them with the back of a knife. Set aside.

4. Season the potatoes with salt and pepper, then heat some oil in a frying pan over a medium to high heat. Add the potatoes and fry until they are golden brown on both sides.

5. Add the crushed garlic cloves and cook for a minute, then add the butter.

6. Once the butter has melted, add the rosemary and thyme, then pour in the chicken stock.

7. Bring to the boil, then transfer the potatoes to the oven and bake for 40 minutes, or until tender. If they start to turn too dark, cover with tin foil.

Tip: You can pop the potato offcuts into water and keep them in the fridge for up to 2 days. You can use these to make mashed potatoes.

CREAMY POTATO SALAD

PREP TIME: 10 MINUTES | COOKING TIME: 15 MINUTES | SERVES: 6

Potato salad is a summer staple at barbecues and picnics, and for a good reason! This classic dish is easy to make, hearty, and satisfying. In this recipe, boiled potatoes are combined with a creamy dressing, and the result is a delicious and comforting side dish.

INGREDIENTS

800g baby potatoes

1 red onion, diced

1 bunch of chives, finely chopped

4 tbsp crème fraiche

4 tbsp mayonnaise

1 tbsp Dijon mustard

1 lemon, zested and juiced

METHOD

1. Start by cutting the baby potatoes into halves or quarters so they're all roughly the same size.

2. Drop them into a pan of salted boiling water and cook until tender.

3. Drain them into a colander and run under cold water until cool.

4. Tip the potatoes into a large mixing bowl and add the red onion, chives, crème fraiche, mayonnaise, mustard and the zest and juice of the lemon.

5. Season with salt and pepper, then stir until well combined.

6. Pile high in a salad bowl and serve alongside a barbecue or summer spread.

CREAMED SPINACH

PREP TIME: 5 MINUTES | COOKING TIME: 10 MINUTES | SERVES: 2

Creamed spinach is a classic side dish that is loved for its rich and creamy texture. Whether you're serving it as a side dish for a holiday meal or just looking for a tasty way to incorporate more greens into your diet, this Creamed Spinach recipe is sure to be a hit.

INGREDIENTS

35g butter

1 onion, diced

4 cloves of garlic, chopped

2 tbsp plain flour

200ml whole milk

400g baby spinach

100ml crème fraiche

40g parmesan, grated

1 tsp ground nutmeg

METHOD

1. Add the butter to a large pan and melt over a medium to high heat. Once melted, add the onion, and cook for 5 minutes until softened.

2. Chuck in the garlic and cook for a further minute, then stir in the plain flour and cook for 2 more minutes.

3. Gradually pour in the milk, whisking continuously until it's been incorporated. Turn the heat down to medium and cook for 5 minutes, stirring occasionally until it thickens.

4. Add the spinach into the sauce – you may have to do this bit by bit.

5. Once all the spinach has wilted, stir through the crème fraiche, parmesan, and nutmeg. Season to taste and dish up.

CHAMP MASH

PREP TIME: 10 MINUTES | COOKING TIME: 20 MINUTES | SERVES: 6

This delicious and creamy Champ Mash is the perfect comfort food. The tender potatoes, rich cream, crispy pancetta, and aromatic spring onions come together to create a side dish that is both satisfying and flavourful. Whether you serve it as a holiday staple or as part of a weeknight dinner, this Champ Mash is sure to become a family favourite.

INGREDIENTS

1.5kg Maris Piper or King Edward potatoes

80g butter

120ml whole milk

100ml double cream

150g pancetta

100g spring onions, sliced

METHOD

1. Peel the potatoes, chop them into even-sized chunks, and place them in a large pot of cold water. Season well with salt.

2. Bring the potatoes to the boil, then turn down the heat slightly to prevent it from overflowing. Cook until the potatoes are tender and can easily be pierced with a knife.

3. Drain them and leave to steam dry.

4. Transfer the potatoes to a pan or mixing bowl and use a potato masher to mash the potatoes to a smooth consistency. Or, for an extra smooth mash, use a potato ricer. Add in the butter and fold it through until it melts.

5. Meanwhile, add the milk and cream into a saucepan and bring it almost to the boil.

6. Pour it into the potatoes and fold it through.

7. Add the pancetta into a dry pan and cook over a high heat until it's nice and crispy.

8. Add the crispy pancetta and sliced spring onions to the mash, fold them through, and serve.

IRRESISTIBLE SWEET TREATS

Talk about saving the best for last! Here's a collection of some of my favourite sweet recipes that are all sure to be showstoppers. Cookies, cakes, tarts, pies and more! I find baking to be a little more of a science compared to the free-spirited nature of cooking, but whether you want to bake for fun, for a special occasion, or to impress your loved ones, there's a wide range of recipes to get you inspired.

SWEET PASTRY

PREP TIME: 10 MINUTES, PLUS 30 MINUTES RESTING | SERVES: 8

Making pastry is notoriously difficult. In most cases, I would recommend that people buy the ready-made pastry from the supermarket; it's affordable and easy to use, and you can even keep it in the freezer and thaw it out quickly when needed. However, this sweet pastry recipe is simple to make, and makes a real difference when making pastry treats. It was one of the first things I learnt to make when I started working towards my NVQ in professional cookery. I was working in the officer's mess in Reading Young Offenders Institute. The officer's mess was basically the staff canteen, and the food generally consisted of basic food like omelettes, chips, casseroles, pies, and soups. There were always two young inmates working there with a lovely local lady called Sue. Each week, she would order in special ingredients so that we could practise making things that we wouldn't usually have been able to make. I fondly remember making the sweet pastry and using it to make all sorts of delights.

INGREDIENTS

250g plain flour

100g icing sugar

125g cold butter, diced

1 egg yolk

METHOD

1. Add the plain flour, icing sugar and butter to a large mixing bowl.

2. Use your fingers to rub the ingredients together until they resemble fine breadcrumbs.

3. Add the egg and mix well, then tip the dough out onto a clean surface and pat together until it forms a dough. If the dough is a little dry, add a teaspoon of water.

4. Wrap the dough in cling film and place it in the fridge for at least 30 minutes to rest.

5. Once rested, it's ready to use. You can also store it in the fridge for 2 to 3 days, or in the freezer for up to a month.

PEAR & FRANGIPANE TART

PREP TIME: 15 MINUTES | COOKING TIME: 1 HOUR 15 MINUTES | SERVES: 8

If you've never heard of frangipane, just think about the cakey part of a Bakewell tart. The moist almond sponge makes a delicious filling for this tart, and when paired with the sweetness of the poached pears, the combination is undeniably delightful.

INGREDIENTS

FOR THE POACHED PEARS

400g granulated sugar

1.4 litres cold water

1 star anise

2 cinnamon sticks

2 lemons, zested and juiced

3 pears

FOR THE FRANGIPANE TART

Sweet Pastry (see page 210)

200g butter, softened

200g caster sugar

140g ground almonds

100g self-raising flour

½ tsp ground cinnamon

2 eggs

1 tsp vanilla extract

1 tbsp dark rum (optional)

METHOD

FOR THE POACHED PEARS

1. Combine the sugar and water in a saucepan. Place it over a medium heat and bring to a simmer, stirring occasionally until the sugar has dissolved. Add the star anise, cinnamon sticks and lemon zest.

2. Peel the pears, then rub with lemon juice to stop them from turning brown. Cut them in half and use a spoon to take out the core. Place the pear halves into the poaching liquid. It should cover the pears.

3. Place over a medium heat and simmer the pears for about 10 minutes until tender. Be careful not to overcook the pears.

4. Turn off the heat and leave the pears to cool in the poaching liquid.

FOR THE FRANGIPANE TART

1. Preheat the oven to 190°c. Using a little flour, roll out the sweet pastry dough to about 3mm thick. Place the pastry over a 23cm loose-bottomed flan tin and press it into the edges.

2. Prick the base with a fork, then cover with baking paper and baking beans or uncooked rice in an even layer.

3. Blind bake the pastry for 15 minutes. Remove the baking beans and paper, then return it to the oven for another 10 minutes. Once golden and crisp, take it out and set aside to cool. Cut away any excess overhanging pastry.

4. To make the frangipane, beat the remaining ingredients together using an electric whisk until you have a cake-like batter. Pour this into the cooled pastry case.

5. Dry the poached pears on kitchen paper and thinly slice them crosswise. Using a spatula, carefully lift each sliced pear half and place on the frangipane, with the narrow end of the pear facing the centre of the tart and fanning the slices apart slightly as you work. Repeat with the remaining pear halves, spacing them evenly around the tart.

6. Bake the tart for 50 minutes until risen, golden and firm to the touch. Serve warm or cold with crème fraiche and a drizzle of honey.

BANOFFEE PIE

PREP TIME: 20 MINUTES, PLUS I HOUR SETTING TIME | SERVES: 8

Invented in 1970, this no-bake dessert combines the delicious flavours of banana and toffee in a rich and creamy pie. The combination of sweet and smooth creates an irresistible dessert that will impress on any occasion. It's truly timeless.

INGREDIENTS

FOR THE BASE

200g digestive biscuits

100g butter

I tbsp light muscovado sugar

FOR THE FILLING

100g butter

100g light muscovado sugar

I x 397g tin of condensed milk

FOR THE TOPPING

4 ripe bananas

400ml double cream

2 tsp vanilla bean paste

50g chocolate, for grating

METHOD

1. Crush the digestive biscuits until they resemble a fine crumb. You can do this in a food processor or by putting them in a sandwich bag and beating with a rolling pin.

2. Melt the butter and sugar in a pan on a low heat. Combine with the crushed biscuits and mix well.

3. Press the biscuit base into the bottom of a greased 20 x 20cm springform tin and place in the fridge while you make the toffee filling.

4. Heat the butter and sugar over a low heat until the sugar has dissolved, stirring occasionally. Add the condensed milk and bring to the boil. Boil for 2 to 3 minutes, stirring continuously until it is dark and golden. Be careful not to let the mixture catch on the bottom.

5. Pour the toffee into the tin and place in the fridge for at least an hour.

6. Once set, slice the bananas into rounds and arrange them neatly on top of the toffee.

7. Whip the cream into soft peaks, then fold the vanilla paste through. Spread the cream over the top of the bananas.

8. Chill until ready to serve.

9. When ready, undo the sides of the springform tin. You may need to run a knife around the edges to loosen it up.

10. Grate the chocolate over the top, cut into portions and serve.

CHUNKY CHOCOLATE CHIP COOKIES

PREP TIME: 10 MINUTES | COOKING TIME: 15 MINUTES | SERVES: 12

I've made a lot of cookies over the last 15 years, but none of them come close to this recipe. These are made using melted butter and are cooked at a lower temp, so the cookie is much cakier than traditional recipes. They're big, thick, and incredibly moreish. Try substituting the chocolate chunks for nuts or pieces of your favourite chocolate bars.

INGREDIENTS

140g butter

120g soft brown sugar

60g granulated sugar

2 tsp vanilla extract

1 egg

340g plain flour

½ tsp bicarbonate of soda

2 tsp baking powder

300g chocolate, cut into chunks

METHOD

1. Preheat the oven to 170°c.

2. Melt the butter in a saucepan over a medium heat.

3. In a large mixing bowl, combine the soft brown sugar, granulated sugar, and melted butter. Whisk together for 4 to 5 minutes until the butter is well combined with the sugar.

4. Add the vanilla extract and the egg and mix well to combine.

5. Combine the flour, bicarbonate of soda, baking powder, and a pinch of salt.

6. Sift the flour into the butter and sugar mixture and use a wooden spoon to mix until a dough has formed.

7. Fold the chocolate chunks through the dough.

8. Roll the cookie dough into a sausage shape, cover with cling film, and place into the fridge for 20 minutes. This will firm it up a little bit.

9. Cut the dough into 12 equal portions, weighing approximately 100g each.

10. Place the cookie dough portions onto lined baking trays, leaving enough space in between so they can spread during baking.

11. Press each cookie down a little bit to make a rough cookie shape.

12. Bake for 13 to 15 minutes until they are golden around the edges.

13. Leave them to cool on the tray for 10 minutes before transferring them to a cooling rack.

Tip: You can freeze the dough and just cut off the cookie dough and bake as and when you want them.

MILLIONAIRE FLAPJACKS

PREP TIME: 15 MINUTES, PLUS 2 HOURS SETTING | MAKES: 9

Whether it's for a bake sale or a treat to share with friends, take this easy 'no bake' flapjack and turn it into the ultimate delicious treat. Sure to be a showstopper!

INGREDIENTS

FOR THE FLAPJACK

100g butter

100g soft brown sugar

55g golden syrup

1 tbsp peanut butter

250g porridge oats

FOR THE CARAMEL

100g butter

100g soft dark brown sugar

1 x 397g tin of condensed milk

FOR THE TOPPING

150g milk chocolate

METHOD

1. For the flapjack, line a 20cm square baking tin with baking paper. In a large saucepan, melt the butter, soft brown sugar, golden syrup, and peanut butter over a medium heat. Stir often to prevent it from burning on the bottom of the pan.

2. Take the mixture off the heat and stir through the porridge oats. Press the mixture firmly into the prepared tin, then pop it into the fridge for at least half an hour to set.

3. For the caramel, melt the butter and sugar over a medium heat. Pour in the condensed milk and mix well.

4. Bring the caramel to the boil, then turn the heat down slightly so it is still bubbling. Stir continuously for 2 to 3 minutes until dark and golden.

5. Pour the caramel over the flapjack. Leave it to cool slightly before placing it into the fridge for about an hour to cool completely.

6. For the topping, melt the chocolate in a heatproof bowl over a pan of simmering water. Pour it over the set caramel and spread it into the edges. Pop the tin into the fridge until the chocolate has set completely.

7. Cut into portions and enjoy. Store at room temperature in an airtight container for up to 5 days.

Tip: When melting the chocolate, make sure the bowl does not touch the water in the pan, otherwise the chocolate will burn.

NO NUT CARROT CAKE

PREP TIME: 20 MINUTES | COOKING TIME: 40 MINUTES | SERVES: 8

This is my favourite recipe for carrot cake; it's super simple to make and really delicious. It's a moist (I know, I hate that word too) sponge, it's full of flavour, and it's topped with a citrusy cream cheese icing. The omission of nuts makes this a safe, allergy-friendly option for your guests… or whoever might try and sneak a slice.

INGREDIENTS

FOR THE CARROT CAKE

180g light muscovado sugar

180ml sunflower oil

4 eggs

150g carrots, grated

100g raisins

1 tsp ground cinnamon

½ tsp ground nutmeg

2 oranges, zested

1 tsp bicarbonate of soda

180g self-raising flour

FOR THE ICING

200g full-fat cream cheese

150g caster sugar

100g butter, softened

1 orange, juiced and zested

METHOD

1. Preheat the oven to 180°c and line a 20cm cake tin.

2. Add the muscovado sugar, sunflower oil and eggs to a large mixing bowl and beat until smooth.

3. Add the grated carrot, raisins, cinnamon, nutmeg, and orange zest. Fold it all together.

4. Combine the bicarbonate of soda and self-raising flour, then sift into the cake batter. Fold together until it's well combined.

5. Pour the batter into the lined cake tin and bake for 40 minutes.

6. When ready, it should be firm and springy in the middle. Leave it to cool in the tin for a few minutes before turning it out onto a wire cooling rack.

7. Prepare the icing by adding the cream cheese, caster sugar, softened butter, and the orange juice into a mixing bowl, then whisk until it's smooth and creamy.

8. Once the cake has cooled, smooth the icing over the top and finish with more orange zest.

9. Pop into the fridge until the icing has set.

Tip: Toss the raisins with a teaspoon of plain flour before adding to the batter. This will prevent them from sinking to the bottom of your cake.

LEMON MERINGUE PIE

PREP TIME: 10 MINUTES | COOKING TIME: 2 HOURS 20 MINUTES | SERVES: 4

One of my favourite things to do is to take a "tricky" recipe and create a simpler version that almost anyone can make. This is my easy Lemon Meringue Pie. It has a buttery digestive base filled with a ridiculously simple lemon curd and is topped with Italian meringue.

INGREDIENTS

FOR THE BASE

300g digestive biscuits

150g butter

FOR THE LEMON FILLING

4 egg yolks

1 x 397g tin of condensed milk

4 lemons, zested and juiced

FOR THE MERINGUE

4 egg whites

1½ tsp cream of tartar

200g caster sugar

100ml water

METHOD

1. Preheat the oven to 140°c.

2. Use a food processor to blitz the digestive biscuits to a fine crumb. Alternatively, place them into a sandwich bag and smash with a rolling pin.

3. Melt the butter and pour it over the crushed biscuits. Mix well until it resembles wet sand.

4. Pour the mixture into an 18cm springform tin. Press it into the edges so that it has a 1 to 2cm high edge.

5. Put it in the fridge while you prepare the filling.

6. Add the egg yolks, condensed milk, and the zest and juice of the lemons to a mixing bowl.

7. Beat with a whisk for a few minutes until completely smooth.

8. Pour the mixture on the digestive base and bake for 15 minutes.

9. Leave to cool at room temperature before placing it into the fridge to set for at least 2 hours.

10. To make the meringue, add the egg whites into a large mixing bowl along with the cream of tartar. Beat with an electric whisk until it makes soft peaks.

11. Meanwhile, add the sugar and water into a saucepan and boil rapidly over a high heat to make a syrup. Use a thermometer to read the temperature – it needs to reach 115°c.

12. Slowly pour the sugar syrup into the egg whites while continually whisking the meringue. Once you've poured all the sugar syrup in, beat the whites on the highest setting until they've stiffened up.

13. Spoon as much as you'd like over the top of the pie, then use a chef's blowtorch to create the golden colour on top. Alternatively, you can pop it under a hot grill until golden.

RETRO CHOCOLATE SCHOOL CAKE

PREP TIME: 10 MINUTES | COOKING TIME: 20 MINUTES | SERVES: 9

I loved the sweet treats we used to get at school – especially the cake with icing and sprinkles. After going viral in 2020 with my School Cake recipe, suddenly celebrity chefs, food bloggers and supermarkets were all celebrating old school puddings. This is my recipe for the chocolate version of School Cake, which is perfect on its own or with loads of custard. YUM!

INGREDIENTS

FOR THE SPONGE

180g caster sugar

180g butter, softened

3 eggs

150g self-raising flour

30g cocoa powder

2 tsp vanilla extract

40ml whole milk

FOR THE TOPPING

360g icing sugar

40g cocoa powder

75ml whole milk

1 tsp vanilla extract

Chocolate sprinkles

METHOD

1. Preheat the oven to 180°c and line a 20 x 20cm baking tin with baking paper.

2. Add the caster sugar and softened butter to a large mixing bowl and beat with a whisk until it starts to turn creamy.

3. Add the eggs, flour, cocoa powder, and vanilla extract and beat until well combined.

4. Add the milk and beat it in. You should now have a smooth cake batter.

5. Pour the mixture into your lined baking tin and smooth it out into the edges.

6. Bake in the oven for 20 minutes. When ready, it should be springy to touch, and if you poke a skewer in the middle, it should come out clean.

7. Leave the cake to cool in the tin for 10 minutes before turning it out onto a cooling rack. Turn it upside down to ensure a flat top.

8. Once it has cooled completely, make the icing. Combine the icing sugar and cocoa powder in a large mixing bowl, then pour in the milk and vanilla extract and whisk together until completely smooth.

9. Spread the icing over the cake and cover with chocolate sprinkles. Leave the icing to set.

10. Cut into nine portions and serve.

THE BEST STICKY TOFFEE PUDDING

PREP TIME: 20 MINUTES | COOKING TIME: 45 MINUTES | SERVES: 9

This is the best of British. Comfort food doesn't get much better than this delicious, moist sponge cake made with finely chopped dates, covered with a rich toffee sauce, and served with ice cream, custard, or crème fraiche.

INGREDIENTS

FOR THE SPONGE PUDDING

200g Medjool dates, pitted

100g butter, softened

180g light muscovado sugar

3 eggs

3 tbsp black treacle

250g self-raising flour

1 tsp baking powder

1 tsp bicarbonate of soda

150ml whole milk

FOR THE TOFFEE SAUCE

100g butter

200g light muscovado sugar

2 tbsp black treacle

400ml double cream

METHOD

1. Preheat the oven to 175°c.

2. Chop the Medjool dates into fine pieces and soak them in 150ml of boiling water for 20 minutes.

3. Meanwhile, add the softened butter, muscovado sugar and eggs into a large mixing bowl. Whisk together for a few minutes until well combined, then add the black treacle and beat together.

4. Sift in the self-raising flour, baking powder and bicarbonate of soda.

5. Use a whisk to combine, then slowly add the milk while mixing continuously.

6. Once the dates have soaked up the water, use a fork to mash them into a paste-like consistency before folding them through the pudding mix.

7. Pour the mixture into a greased 20 x 20cm tray and bake in the oven for 30 to 35 minutes.

8. Meanwhile, prepare the toffee sauce. Add the butter and muscovado sugar into a large pan over a low heat and slowly melt together.

9. Add the black treacle and half of the cream.

10. Turn to a medium to high heat and bubble for 2 to 3 minutes, stirring continuously.

11. Take off the heat, add the remaining cream, and beat until combined.

12. Once the sponge has cooked, take it out and leave to cool for about 20 minutes. Cut into portions then pour two thirds of the sauce over the top. You can serve immediately with the remaining sauce on top or leave it like this at room temperature for up to 2 days.

13. If reheating, warm through in a hot oven for a few minutes until the sauce is bubbling and sticky. Heat the remaining sauce and pour it over the pudding. Serve with your choice of ice cream, custard, or crème fraiche.

THE ULTIMATE TRIPLE CHOCOLATE BROWNIES

PREP TIME: 10 MINUTES | COOKING TIME: 25 MINUTES | SERVES: 12

You will never need another chocolate brownie recipe after trying this one. The secret with these is to take them out of the oven when they still look under-baked. Then, once cool, pop them in the fridge. They are the most delicious, fudgiest brownies you'll ever eat.

INGREDIENTS

200g butter

200g dark chocolate (70% cocoa)

3 eggs, plus 1 egg yolk

300g golden caster sugar

100g plain flour

50g cocoa powder

150g chocolate chips (50g each of white, milk, and dark)

METHOD

1. Preheat the oven to 165°c.

2. Cut the butter into chunks and place in a heatproof bowl along with the dark chocolate.

3. Melt over a pan of simmering water until smooth, then take off the heat and set aside to cool slightly.

4. Use an electric whisk to beat the eggs, egg yolk and sugar until it is pale and thick. It should double in size.

5. Pour the melted chocolate and butter into the egg and sugar mixture and fold through. Be careful not to knock the air out of it. Use the figure of eight method, going around and under.

6. Sift the flour and cocoa into the mixture.

7. Fold together to incorporate, then fold through the chocolate chips.

8. Pour the fudgy mixture into a lined baking tray (a 20 x 30cm one is best) and spread into the corners of the tray.

9. Bake for 22 to 25 minutes. It should have a slight wobble in the middle and will have formed a paper-like crust.

10. Leave to cool until it's reached room temperature. I like to put it in the fridge for a few hours before cutting it into portions.

11. Serve at room temperature.

FRUIT & NUT FLAPJACKS

PREP TIME: 10 MINUTES | COOKING TIME: 30 MINUTES | SERVES: 9

This is my go-to recipe for the ULTIMATE flapjacks. It's a little more effort than a no-bake recipe, but the sweet, slightly salted, crunchy edges of the flapjack make it all worthwhile. Chocolate is usually the best way to entice people into baking but trust me when I say you need to make these!

INGREDIENTS

200g butter

200g light muscovado sugar

80g honey

1 tsp salt

120g mixed dried fruit

80g pistachios, chopped

380g rolled porridge oats

METHOD

1. Preheat the oven to 160°c. Grease and line a 20 x 20cm baking tin.

2. Place the butter, sugar, honey, and salt into a large pan over a medium heat. Stir occasionally until the butter has melted.

3. Add the fruit and nuts and stir to combine.

4. Add the oats and mix until well incorporated. Transfer the mixture to the prepared tin and press down into the edges.

5. Bake it for 30 minutes or until golden around the edges. It will look soft when you take it out, but it will firm up as it cools.

6. Leave to cool completely then cut into squares.

CINNAMON ROLLS

These gorgeous cinnamon rolls are perfect for beginners. They're extra soft, have a delicious swirl and, better yet, they freeze well so they're perfect for making ahead!

INGREDIENTS

FOR THE DOUGH

400g plain flour

60g golden caster sugar

Pinch of salt

180ml whole milk

50g butter

7g sachet of dried yeast

1 egg

FOR THE FILLING

75g butter, softened

100g soft brown sugar

1 tbsp ground cinnamon

FOR THE ICING

200g cream cheese

50g butter, softened

100g icing sugar

1 tsp vanilla extract

1 orange, zested

METHOD

1. Add the flour, sugar and a pinch of salt to a large mixing bowl and whisk together.

2. Add the milk and butter to a saucepan and heat until the butter has melted, making sure not to boil the milk. Once melted, take it off the heat.

3. Add the yeast to the milk and whisk until dissolved.

4. Pour the milk into the dry ingredients, add the egg, then stir well with a wooden spoon. Mix until a soft dough forms.

5. Transfer the dough to a lightly floured surface, then knead the dough for a few minutes. If the dough feels too sticky, add a little flour.

6. When you have a soft, smooth dough, set it aside to prove for 30 minutes while you get the filling ready.

7. For the filling, mix the sugar, softened butter, and cinnamon together.

8. Once proved, roll the dough into a rectangle that's about 0.5cm thick, spread the filling all over, then roll the dough into a log shape.

9. Cut the log into 12 equal-sized rolls and space them evenly within a large baking dish. Cover with cling film and leave the rolls to double in size. This should take about 45 minutes.

10. Preheat the oven to 190°c.

11. Bake the cinnamon rolls for 25 minutes or until lightly browned. Remove from the oven and set aside.

12. Add the cream cheese and softened butter to a large mixing bowl and beat until smooth and creamy. Then, add the icing sugar, vanilla, the zest of the orange and the juice of half of the orange. Beat until smooth, then spread the icing over the cinnamon rolls.

13. Enjoy right away, or store at room temperature in an airtight container for up to 2 days, or in the fridge for up to 5 days.

CUSTARD TART

PREP TIME: 20 MINUTES | COOKING TIME: 1 HOUR 10 MINUTES | SERVES: 8

This is very similar to the Portuguese pasteis de nata which are usually small individual tarts. I've made this recipe as simple as possible while keeping that authentic Portuguese custard tart taste.

INGREDIENTS

320g ready-rolled puff pastry

1 egg white, beaten

50g plain flour

260ml whole milk

6 egg yolks

2 tsp vanilla bean paste

150ml water

250g golden caster sugar

1 cinnamon stick

TO SERVE

Icing sugar

Ground cinnamon

Crème fraiche

Fresh raspberries

METHOD

1. To make the pastry base, preheat the oven to 200°c. Gently lay the pastry sheet into a 20cm shallow cake tin, pressing it down gently and making sure it overhangs the edges. If needed, you can remove excess pastry from the overhang and use it to fill any gaps.

2. Prick the pastry base with a fork, then cover with baking paper and fill with baking beans. Bake in the preheated oven for 20 minutes.

3. Remove the beans and baking paper, brush the pastry case with the egg white, then bake for a further 10 minutes. Remove and leave to cool slightly. Keep the oven on.

4. For the custard filling, put the plain flour and milk into a saucepan, then whisk until smooth. Cook over a medium heat, whisking often, until it thickens. Once thickened, take it off the heat and beat in the egg yolks and vanilla bean paste. Set aside.

5. In another saucepan, combine the water, golden caster sugar and cinnamon stick. Cook over a medium-high heat until it reaches boiling point.

6. Remove the cinnamon stick, then slowly pour the sugar syrup into the milk mixture while whisking continuously. It should be a very runny consistency.

7. Pour the custard into the pastry case and then bake for 35 to 40 minutes or until set with a slight wobble in the centre.

8. Heat the grill to high, then grill the tart for 2 to 3 minutes until blackened and blistered on top. Leave to cool slightly before sprinkling with icing sugar and ground cinnamon.

9. Serve in slices with a dollop of crème fraiche and some raspberries.

Tip: You can freeze the leftover egg whites to be used another time.

CHOCOLATE TART

PREP TIME: 20 MINUTES, PLUS 3 HOURS SETTING TIME | SERVES: 8

Use my easy sweet pastry recipe to create this rich chocolate tart. This is a great recipe to make ahead of time, and it's sure to impress on any occasion. Top with raspberries and pistachios and serve with a dollop of crème fraiche.

INGREDIENTS

Sweet Pastry (see page 210)

300g dark chocolate (70% cocoa)

100g milk chocolate

2 tbsp honey

300ml double cream

100g butter

1 tsp vanilla bean paste

TO SERVE (OPTIONAL)

25g pistachios, chopped

150g raspberries

Crème fraiche

METHOD

1. Preheat the oven to 190°c.

2. Using a little flour, roll out the sweet pastry dough to about 3mm thick. Place the pastry over the top of a 23cm loose-bottomed flan tin and press it into the edges.

3. Prick the base with a fork, then place baking paper over the top. Add baking beans (or rice) and give the tin a shake so they spread evenly across the pastry.

4. Blind bake for 15 minutes. Then, remove the baking beans and the baking paper and return it to the oven for another 10 minutes. Once it's golden and crisp, take it out and set aside to cool. Cut away any excess overhanging pastry.

5. Chop the milk and dark chocolate into small pieces, then add to a large mixing bowl along with the honey.

6. Add the double cream, butter and vanilla bean paste to a saucepan and simmer over a medium heat until the butter has melted. Then pour the hot cream over the chocolate.

7. Use a whisk to beat until smooth and glossy.

8. Pour the mixture over the pastry base and leave to cool to room temperature before placing into the fridge to set. This will take about 3 hours.

9. Sprinkle with the chopped pistachio and serve with raspberries and a spoonful of crème fraiche.

Tip: Warm your knife with hot water before cutting it for a clean cut.

CHURROS

PREP TIME: 15 MINUTES | COOKING TIME: 10 MINUTES | SERVES: 8

Crisp pastry dusted with cinnamon sugar and served with a rich chocolate sauce is always such a treat. Whenever I go to food festivals or street fairs, the queues for the churros are always huge, but here's how to make your very own at home.

INGREDIENTS

FOR THE CHOCOLATE SAUCE

120g dark chocolate (70% cocoa)

240ml double cream

FOR THE CINNAMON SUGAR

2 tsp ground cinnamon

50g caster sugar

FOR THE CHURROS

240ml water

90g butter

15g caster sugar

120g plain flour

2 eggs

Neutral cooking oil, for frying

METHOD

FOR THE CHOCOLATE SAUCE

1. Chop the chocolate into small pieces and place in a bowl.

2. Heat the double cream until almost boiling, then pour it over the chocolate and whisk until smooth and glossy.

FOR THE CINNAMON SUGAR AND CHURROS

1. Mix the cinnamon and caster sugar together and set aside.

2. For the churro dough, add the water, butter and sugar into a saucepan and bring to a boil.

3. Once boiling, take it off the heat and beat all the flour in at once. Beat well for about 2 minutes until it's well incorporated.

4. Return the pan to the heat and cook for a further 30 seconds, stirring continuously. This is a key step that will make the mixture a little dryer.

5. Take it off the heat again and gradually beat the eggs in one at a time. Mix until the dough is smooth, thick, and glossy.

6. Half fill a large pot with oil and bring to temperature, ready to deep fry. If you have a thermometer, the oil should be at 190°c. If you don't, dip the end of a wooden spoon into the oil and if bubbles form around it, then it's up to temperature.

7. Spoon the dough into a piping bag, ideally with a large star tip to get the authentic churro shape. Pipe six-inch pieces into the hot oil and fry for 90 seconds to 2 minutes until they are golden brown. Do three or four at a time for best results.

8. Remove the churros and transfer to kitchen paper to get rid of any excess oil.

9. While warm, toss the churros in a bowl with the cinnamon sugar. Serve with the chocolate sauce.

First edition printed in 2023 in the UK

ISBN: 978-1-915538-06-2

Written by: Jon Watts

Edited by: Emily Readman & Katie Fisher

Photography by: Timm Cleasby
(www.timmcleasby.com)

Designed by: Paul Cocker, Sam Borland
& Rhianna Emberson

Sales & PR: Emma Toogood & Lizzy Capps

Contributors: Lis Ellis & Phil Turner

Printed by: Bell & Bain Ltd, UK

MIX
Paper | Supporting
responsible forestry
FSC® C007785

Published by Meze Publishing Limited

Unit 1b, 2 Kelham Square

Kelham Riverside

Sheffield S3 8SD

Web: www.mezepublishing.co.uk

Telephone: 0114 275 7709

Email: info@mezepublishing.co.uk